What Others Are Saying About Anne Peters and This Book

"In *Finding Your Hope*, Anne Peters helps victims of child sexual abuse know it was not their fault and they are not to blame. That is so important. She also provides several helpful resources that can guide you through the healing process. I highly recommend this book if you've been a victim of child sexual abuse, or if you know someone who needs help toward their healing."

— Mary West, The Mary West Network

"After watching my mom heal from chemical sensitivity that had its roots in repressed memories of childhood sexual and physical abuse, I know that resolving those traumas is critical for long-term health. Any sexual abuse survivor will want to refer back to *Finding Your Hope* over and over. It is full of helpful information for healing."

— Robin Lee, Health and Longevity Coach and Author of *Achieving Health and Longevity: The Artful Pursuit of Wellness and Vitality*

"This book can help trauma survivors go from low self-esteem to being ready to face the world. *Finding Your Hope* is a must buy for anyone who is ready to heal from their sexual traumas."

— John Webster, Author of *Mastering Your Fate*

"*Finding Your Hope* offers a comprehensive guide to working through all the stages of sexual abuse from initial diagnosis to complete healing. Prepare to let go of shame and guilt while embracing the freedom of self-forgiveness and experience the limitless possibilities of whom you were meant to be."

— Mia S. Tepper, MBA, Author of *Parenting Pressures and Pleasures: Tips for Each Stage in Your Child's Life*

"From understanding what happened and letting go of shame to even confronting abusers, *Finding Your Hope* outlines a way that survivors can regain their self-esteem. Anne Peters shares her compassion, life experience, and guidance with others who are enduring personal struggles. Definitely a valuable resource for beginning your healing journey."

— Tiiu Napp, Coach, Speaker, and Author of *Healing the Holes in Your Soul*

"From celebrities' stories to her own story, Anne Peters reveals that no one is immune from sexual traumas. No matter who you are, Anne provides concrete and useful tools so you can heal your past, present, and future."

— Brent Scarpo, Life Coach, Speaker, and Author of *The Red Balloon: Transforming Your Life One Story at a Time*

"*Finding Your Hope* is a must have for anyone who has experienced sexual trauma. It's full of inspirational stories, resources, advice, and exercises. Any sexual abuse survivor will want to refer back to this healing book over and over. It is full of helpful information."

— Karie Cassell, Dietitian, Life Coach, and International Bestselling Author of *The Domino Diet: How to Heal You from the Inside Out*

"Being abused does not determine your destiny. The abuse was not your fault and you don't have to let it define you. In *Finding Your Hope*, Anne Peters shows how you can take back your power to create your own destiny. Healing and happiness are possible—make them your destiny."

— Patrick Snow, Publishing Coach and International Bestselling Author of *Creating Your Own Destiny* and *The Affluent Entrepreneur*

"Anyone looking for hope will find it in Anne Peters' new book. Anne shares stories of how she and others have overcome abuse and how healing is possible for anyone. You just have to be willing to do the work and know that as scary as that work may seem, it is doable and a better life awaits you on the other side. In *Finding Your Hope*, you have a step-by-step guide to healing that will help countless people, yourself included."

— Tyler R. Tichelaar, PhD and Award-Winning Author of *Narrow Lives* and *The Best Place*

A PERSONAL GUIDE TO YOUR HEALING PROCESS

Finding Your Hope

Restoring Peace in Life After Sexual Abuse

ANNE PETERS
SURVIVOR

FINDING YOUR HOPE
Restoring Peace in Life After Sexual Abuse

Published by:
Aviva Publishing
Lake Placid, NY
(518) 523-1320
www.AvivaPubs.com

Anne Peters
(253) 225-3380
annepeters@findingyourhope.com
www.FindingYourHope.com
www.AnnePetersCoaching.com

ISBN: 978-1-63618-159-2
Library of Congress Control Number: 2021921846

Editor: Tyler Tichelaar, Superior Book Productions
Cover Designer: Fusion Creative Works
Interior Book Fusion Creative Works
Cover Photo: Anne Peters, Peters Art & Design
Author Photo: Darcy Howell

Every attempt has been made to properly source all quotes.

Printed in the United States of America

First Edition

2 4 6 8 10 12

For my husband, Timothy,

Without your support, this book never would have happened.

For my children and grandchildren,

Chris, Jessica, Avianna, James, Adelyn, and Harper, I hope you never to have to go through what I have been through.

For my parents,

You have always loved and believed in me.

For all my extended family

and all the lives they have touched along the way.

And finally,

for the future generations who may benefit from this book.

Acknowledgments

I would like to acknowledge two incredibly rare friends of mine.

First, Mary West, an awesome networker, for introducing me to Patrick Snow.

Secondly, Patrick Snow for encouraging and helping me to write and publish this book.

Without either of them, this book would not have been possible.

Contents

Introduction

Breaking Free

"Never let someone else's opinion become your reality."

— Les Brown

"1 in 5 girls and 1 in 20 boys is a victim of child sexual abuse. A child who is the victim of prolonged sexual abuse usually develops low self-esteem, a feeling of worthlessness and an abnormal or distorted view of sex. The child may become withdrawn and mistrustful of adults and can become suicidal."[1]

I am sure a certain percentage of people never admit to being victims of sexual abuse because they are embarrassed or humiliated by it. Some may stay silent because of fear. Have you ever thought you might have been sexually abused? Or do you know you were sexually abused? Are you dealing with feelings of shame and guilt? Perhaps you know someone or live with someone who has been abused.

I have been there. I have been sexually abused and molested by a close family friend. I have also been molested by a supposedly trusted figure of authority, and again by a total stranger. None of these events were reported at the time of the incident. I kept all of them secret for many years, even decades. Why? Shame and embarrassment. I had such low self-esteem that I thought I was worthless. Only much later in life did I learn that was not true. Eventually, my insatiable curiosity took over and I tried to find out why I was so different. After all my research into psychology and human behavior, I discovered I was not so different, just influenced by what had happened to me as a child. Sexual abuse victims often think of themselves as "damaged goods," and they feel they do not deserve love. They often feel stuck in a life they cannot escape.

In this book, you will learn how to determine if you were sexually abused, to what degree, and whether you can prosecute or just confront. You will also learn how to locate useful resources for your own healing process, how to determine whether to try counseling or therapy, and how to choose a counselor or therapist. I will also help you find healthier ways to release your emotions and cope with life's frustrations. I mainly want to help people who have been victimized by relatives or authority figures. I want victims to know it was not their fault and they are not to blame.

I wrote this book to help people speak out for themselves and get help if they need it. You do not have to stay silent anymore. Talk to someone you trust. "Trust" I know is a sticky subject for those who really were victimized; you do not trust people easily, if at all. You may automatically expect the worst of everyone until you have known them for a little while. That is okay because it is better to get to know someone before you let your guard down. I felt worthless because of what happened to me, but I should not have. What happened to me was not my fault, and I want others who were abused to know it was not their fault either. Do not waste time feeling like a nobody—you are somebody, and you *can* make something good of yourself if you just try. Ask about statutes of limitations—if someone has hurt you, you may still be able to prosecute.

If you apply the strategies I have outlined for you in this book, you, too, can have hope for your future. You *can* have a loving and fulfilled life. You do have value and something to contribute to the world. You, too, can have a happy and satisfied relationship with yourself and with those you love and live with. You can learn to recognize unhealthy relationships and avoid getting involved with people it might not be in your best interest to be around.

I know you are probably thinking you may never get over what happened to you, but you *can*. Just take a deep breath, put one foot in front of the other, and take it one step at a time. Please keep in mind as you read that certain things may trigger you. A "trigger" is anything that reminds you of traumatic events from the past that lead to a mental, physical, or emotional reaction in the present moment. If you start to feel triggered, put down this book for a while and distract yourself with something else. Come back to it later when you feel more relaxed.

To make it easier, less emotional, and to reduce the possibility of triggers, I hope you will use this book like a workbook.

I recommend that you read through the book first. Then go back and start the exercises. Starting at the beginning is best, but you can start working on the exercises anywhere in the book. Some of these topics will be difficult, so take your time to think about what you read, or reread a chapter before moving on to the next one. Take everything at your own pace and do what feels best for you. There is nothing wrong with jumping back and forth in the chapters if you feel more comfortable working that way. After all, that is how I wrote the book—I wrote the sections I felt inspired to write at the time and then eventually put it all together. It doesn't matter how you do it or in what order, so long as in the long run, you can put it all together to put you all together again, and I know you can!

Finally, before we begin, let me say I am proud of you for picking up this book and beginning this journey. I know that revisiting your past can be scary. That is understandable. But I promise you that a better life awaits you at the end of this journey, so I invite you to take this journey with me.

Let's begin.

Anne Peters

Chapter 1

Understanding What Happened

"I want, by understanding myself, to understand others. I want to be all that I am capable of becoming."

— Katherine Mansfield

With this first chapter, we will dive deeply into this book's subject. Some of the chapter subtitles may be a little intense, but you must understand what happened to you to heal and move on. I will help guide you through the process. These subjects may bring up strong emotions, so be prepared. In this chapter, you will learn about how perpetrators use pornography to entice and lure their victims into sexual acts that the victims would not ordinarily do. Also, how perpetrators threaten or shame their victims into silence. You will learn what "grooming" means.

DISCOVERING PORNOGRAPHY

When you were a child, did anyone ever show you any kind of pornography? Was this person older than you? Was this person being unusually nice to you, or acting slightly out of character? Did it make you feel "icky," "dirty," or extremely uncomfortable? Chances are that person was "grooming" you for a future encounter that might become sexual.

What does grooming mean? Grooming is the process by which an offender draws a victim into a sexual relationship and maintains that relationship in secrecy. In this grooming process, you may have been exposed to pornography by having an older individual or family member show it to you. Perhaps you were convinced or enticed into doing something you would not ordinarily have done.

Different law enforcement officers and academics have proposed models of the "stages" of grooming. Since there are various models, it is best to think of grooming by sex offenders as a gradual, calculated process that ensnares children into a world in which they are, ultimately, willing participants in the sexual abuse. On Oprah.com, forensic psychiatrist Dr. Michael Welner explains six stages that can lead to sexual molestation. Those stages are:

Stage 1: Targeting the victim

Stage 2: Gaining the victim's trust

Stage 3: Filling a need

Stage 4: Isolating the child

Stage 5: Sexualizing the relationship

Stage 6: Maintaining control

As you can see, this is a slow process—so much so that the victim may not even realize it is happening.

To learn more details about this process, please visit:

https://www.oprah.com/oprahshow/child-sexual-abuse-6-stages-of-grooming/.

GETTING EXPOSED

Let me tell you a story about my first encounter with pornography. I was about ten or eleven when a close family friend broke into a locked filing cabinet that contained some very graphic pornography. They were mostly black and white photos that had been printed in some newsprint magazine. This person was someone I looked up to and always wanted to "play" with or spend time with. He must have sensed this and obviously took advantage of me.

Children will explore their sexuality at an early age. As toddlers, they will touch themselves constantly. None of that is anything sexual; it's just exploring themselves. In preschool, they may start noticing differences between genders and want to explore that. This is where boundaries need to be set. Children are very impressionable, and unless specific boundaries are explained to them about their bodies, they may explore in a way that is unhealthy. State those boundaries in a language they can understand. I told my kids, "Your privates are private. No one can touch you there!"

How old were you when you first encountered sexual abuse? Were you a child, a teenager, an adult? How did it make you feel? Did you tell anyone? If so, why or why not? On the next page, write down your experiences, how young you were, and the emotions you felt. What did you do about it at the time and why?

BEING LURED, PERSUADED, AND ENTICED

For me, the sexual abuse started out very innocently, but eventually, it became somewhat of an obsession for my perpetrator. As a child, have you ever been lured, bribed, or enticed to do something you would not ordinarily do? Afterward, did it make you feel ashamed? This situation happens for children more often than you might think. Most of the time, it goes unreported because of embarrassment and shame. First, my perpetrator bribed me into trying some of the stuff in the photos. He told me he would let me hang out with him and play with his toys and trainset if I would touch him sexually. I did not have any sisters and few close friends, so I felt lonely most of the time. Therefore, I agreed to his request. Then he started to touch me in places I had not been touched before. Surprisingly, my body responded. This response is normal for our bodies, even when we are young, but I did not know that as a child, so I just felt weird and not normal. Still, I liked how it made me feel. Soon, I wanted to experience it again, and at the same time, I thought, *How gross!* As in Stage 3, he was filling a need for me—my need to be included.

KEEPING SECRETS AND RECEIVING THREATS

I feel secrets and threats go hand and hand. Has any adult asked you to keep a secret? Doing so is wrong on many levels. An adult should never ask a child to keep a secret, let alone threaten them with any kind of harm. I was told I had to keep what happened a secret. My perpetrator said things to me like "It's just as much your fault as mine, so you better not say anything." I believed him. Dr. Welner, referring to Stage 6, says, "Once the sex abuse is occurring, offenders commonly use secrecy and blame to maintain the child's continued participation and silence—particularly because the sexual activity may cause the child to withdraw from the relationship."

I would like to share Angie's story with you. Hers is more intense than mine. At eight years old, she was molested by her second stepfather. She suffered beatings and physical and mental abuse. Also, she was abused by his brother and sister. She was raped by multiple people multiple times. Then at age nineteen, she was kidnapped and held for ransom. During that time, she was raped repeatedly and suffered more mental and physical abuse. This all sounds awful, and I am sure it was. I will share with you later in this book what she did to overcome it.

SUMMARY

In this chapter, we learned how perpetrators entice their victims into doing things they would not ordinarily do. After the sexual act, they threaten them into secrecy. The victim begins to feel hopeless about the situation and withdraws from certain relationships. What is especially hard for a victim is if the perpetrator is a close family member, especially one they must live with. By gaining their trust and fulfilling a need, a perpetrator gets close to their victim.

This makes it difficult to do anything to defend themselves. Privacy is nonexistent.

You may have experienced strong emotions during this chapter, and that is okay. It is normal and part of the grieving process. We will talk more about grief later in Chapter 5.

In the next chapter, we will explore how to locate helpful resources such as useful books, remove bad influences, find supportive people, create a supportive environment, and insist on privacy. These are some of the resources you can use to guide you through the healing process. Some of the books I have chosen I have also read. Others I have researched by reading reviews to decide if they are acceptable. I will also guide you in the process of finding supportive people and help you determine whether to put them on your list. In this chapter, you learned about what happened to you; in the next chapter, you will learn to find helpful resources with my guidance. Remember, this healing process is going to take some time and hard work. It will not be easy, and you may experience some flashbacks or repressed memories. Just know that in the end it will have all been worth it.

1. How did you feel when reading this chapter?

2. What new insights did you discover about yourself while working through this chapter?

3. What new discoveries about others and the world around you did you find?

4. What do you plan on doing next or doing differently in the future?

Chapter 2

Locating Helpful Resources

"Start doing what is necessary; then do what is possible; and suddenly you are doing the impossible."

— Francis of Assisi

In the last chapter, we learned about how perpetrators lure their victims into doing things they would not ordinarily do. After the sexual act, they threaten them into secrecy. The victim begins to feel hopeless about the situation and withdraws from certain relationships. We found out how hard it is for a victim if the perpetrator is a close family member, especially one they must live with. By gaining their trust and fulfilling a need, perpetrators get close to their victims.

In this chapter, we will explore useful resources for your healing process. These resources will include choosing books that can guide you in your healing beyond my suggestions. You will also learn how to remove the bad or negative influences that hold you back from your true calling. I will help you decide which people in your life will be supportive and which ones you should avoid. We will explore how to create a supportive environment, one you can make yourself feel comfortable and relaxed enough in that it will help your healing process. Lastly, we will talk about the importance of your privacy when healing. Privacy is essential for anyone going through any kind of healing process, especially an emotional one.

CHOOSING BOOKS ON THE SUBJECT

I have always had an interest in psychology, so I began to search for books I could read. One book recommended to me was *The Courage to Heal* by Ellen Bass and Laura Davis. Because it is a thick book that would have been expensive to purchase, I checked it out from the local library. It has a companion workbook that I eventually decided to purchase, which was a good decision. I had the chance to work through my issues in a way that made sense. I also asked my therapist if I could borrow a few books from his library. Your therapist may not allow this, but I am sure they will steer you in the right direction for where to find helpful books on surviving sexual abuse. Other books that may help you in your healing process are *Homecoming: Reclaiming and Healing Your Inner Child* and *Healing the Shame That Binds You*, both by John Bradshaw.

While doing research for this book, I stumbled upon a couple of more books that could be useful for your healing: *Why Me? Help for Victims of Child Sexual Abuse* by Dr.

Lynn Daugherty, and *Secret Survivors: Uncovering Incest and Its Aftereffects in Women* by E. Sue Blume. I also found a children's book that may be useful when talking about the subject with young children: *Some Secrets Should Never be Kept* by Jayneen Sanders.

REMOVING BAD INFLUENCES

Have you ever thought that some of the people you hang out with or some of the things you do may be holding you back from your potential? Are there any people in your life who just seem to be extremely negative, always complaining about someone or something? You need to limit the amount of time you spend with these kinds of people. They will sap your energy, lower your self-esteem, and create in you a general feeling of unease when you are around them. Also, stop watching movies or TV shows that remind you of what happened. Until you get the help you need to feel better about yourself, do not re-expose yourself to this kind of violence. Besides, who wants to deal with flashbacks? They are no fun.

Have you ever wished you knew why you do certain things to undermine your success, whether at work, in school, or in your personal relationships? These behaviors come from the things we learned when we were abused. They became our normal, no matter how twisted the behavior might be. We did not know any better. I always wondered myself why I sometimes engage in self-defeating behaviors. As these behaviors became our normal, we formed bad habits. Now we have to learn to break them and replace them with good habits. You may even have to move out of your current neighborhood if the area and the people are keeping you down. If the place harbors bad memories, move out! Find a new place to make new, happy memories. If the people in your neighborhood are perpetuating your bad habits, move away!

BEWARE OF ABUSIVE RELATIONSHIPS

I've added this section because it is particularly important for you to know that abusive relationships can kill! I am not kidding. I have an awesome friend, whom I will refer to as "Carissa," who is a domestic violence advocate and a survivor herself. In a recent interview, she explained to me her domestic violence situation and how she got herself and her daughter free from it. Here and throughout this book I will share with you some of my interview with her. Here is the beginning of it.

> **Anne:** Carissa, will you introduce yourself? Tell us about your titles, degrees, passions, and callings.
>
> **Carissa:** I have a vocational/technical degree in broadcast journalism and am working on a bachelor of arts in communication media with a minor in film. I have always been a good student, including graduating cum laude in 1990 with my vocational degree and being named a President's Scholar and Dean's Scholar, and I was a member of the Phi Theta Kappa National Honor Society and Tau Sigma National Honor Society.

In addition, I was always passionate about participating in virtual beauty pageants and have won numerous titles at local, state, national, and international levels, including as Ms. Russia, the name I chose to compete under because of my Russian ethnicity.

Anne: How do you define domestic violence?

Carissa: It's a pattern of power and control used to gain or maintain dominance by one partner over another, in a dating or committed relationship. It goes far beyond physical and sexual violence and includes manipulation and emotional, financial, and spiritual abuse. The underlying concepts used in this definition were created by experts in the field to describe the core issue. More than a year ago, the Trump administration quietly, and without warning, redefined domestic violence to include only physical violence that left marks. Those of us working on this issue are aware that this redefining set us back more than fifty years. It continues to allow victims to be exposed to such things as internal injuries and head injuries that can and do kill, but are not always visible on the outside. Suicide and substance abuse are also often linked to domestic violence because they are ways the victim tries to stop the abuse and find peace or at least forget. Put simply, the redefinition has resulted in more victims being unable to get out safely...and a murder rate that is now at four victims per day and continuing to rise.

Anne: Will you share your own background in relation to domestic abuse?

Carissa: I was with my ex for eight years. I met him at one of the lowest points in my life, when I was most vulnerable. He challenged me, made me laugh, and in the beginning, we had a good friendship. The abuse happened slowly over time. An appropriate analogy would be boiling a live frog: you put it on the stove in a pot of cool water and turn the burner on low, raising the temperature slowly so the frog does not realize what is happening until the water is nearly boiling. If there is no lid, the frog can jump out…but being trapped ("with the lid on") or being ignorant can kill. That is true for both the frog in the analogy and victims of abuse. This is one reason victims stay in abuse. They do not realize what they are experiencing is not just a warm pond until the heat is life threatening. Abuse is not a single event. It is ongoing and starts and stops depending on the moment.

In my case, I was undergoing verbal abuse nearly from the beginning. Each time, I would tell him to stop, but he refused to listen. He allowed me no boundaries and began punching and kicking me before too long, telling me he was teaching me to defend myself. "Play fighting." (There is no such thing!) At night, there was sexual abuse and an ongoing lack of sleep that made my resistance lower. There was financial abuse, as well, and a huge imbalance in power when it comes to money coming in. He would judge if I really "needed" something. While I had a small income of my own, it was spent on house maintenance and other obligations, even though, looking at what he made as a computer systems analyst working for large well-known companies, he would have been considered upper middle class without my income. I did not know how much he was bringing in until a few months before I left.

I had been told for fifteen years I had a better chance of winning the lottery than of having a child. When I got pregnant with my daughter, I had hyperemesis gravidarum, and dropped sixty pounds. I was on total bed rest except when I went to the doctor because I could not even keep water down. When they told me I was pregnant, I felt it was a miracle. I was terrified, but once I heard my daughter's heartbeat, I knew we would be okay. My ex accused me of sleeping around (which was ludicrous) before seeming to accept the situation. He lived in his own little world, though.... It was a high-risk pregnancy, and I was having problems all nine months. She tried to come early.

My daughter was jaundiced and had to sit under Bili lights. The doctors were not sure until the last day if she would be going home with me, or if I would need to come back every day. We were finally released and headed home. She ended up having a significant failure to thrive. (I had to take her in to her pediatrician every day to be weighed to make sure she was maintaining her

> weight.) She also had severe GERD (gastroesophageal reflux disease). She would throw up breastmilk, drenching herself, me, and everything within ten feet. Doctors told me she was having to take in twice the normal amount of milk just to maintain her weight. Years later, I learned that failure to thrive occurs in much higher numbers in births where domestic violence is present.

We'll come back to more of Carissa's story later because she has useful and important information for those who may still be in a dangerous situation.

FINDING SUPPORTIVE PEOPLE

Have you ever thought to yourself, *I need new friends; these jerks don't really care about me*? I have. Once I overheard part of a conversation just as I was getting ready to knock on a friend's door. It was half of a conversation; my friend was on the phone with someone else, talking about me. I got an earful. That day, I realized exactly how she felt about me, and it was not good. So, she stopped being my friend from that point on. Let me rephrase my previous question: Have you ever had a strange gut feeling about a person who might be a friend of yours? Something that did not quite feel right? Listen to the gut feeling; it is trying to tell you something. Surround yourself with people you trust. Find people who believe in and support you. Chances are you may know someone else who has been sexually abused much like yourself. You could be support for each other.

In the space below, make a two-column list of people in your life. One column is for the non-supportive people and the other is for the supportive people. Consider removing the non-supportive people from your life.

____________________	____________________
____________________	____________________
____________________	____________________
____________________	____________________
____________________	____________________
____________________	____________________
____________________	____________________
____________________	____________________
____________________	____________________
____________________	____________________

CREATING A SUPPORTIVE ENVIRONMENT

Make sure you have a safe and nurturing environment to do your healing. Feeling safe is foundational to the human spirit. It is always the basic right of every child to be safe. It is usually the responsibility of the parent or guardian to protect this child. There may have been times in your life when you were not as safe as you should have been. Surround yourself with things and people who make you feel good.

Use positive affirmations; hang or post them in places you frequent, and read them every day. Write things like: I am worthy, I am valuable, I am loved, I am important, etc. I realize you may not believe those things right now, but if you keep reading them, soon you will. If you work or take care of children, make sure you schedule time for your healing processes. Perhaps set up a time when a friend or family member can watch your children so you have some uninterrupted time to do your healing work.

When furnishing your environment, you may want to consider using a weighted blanket. They have been known to ease anxiety and comfort people experiencing stress. The weight has a calming effect on the individual. Keep your surrounding clear of clutter. A messy environment can also make you feel anxious. If you can repaint your surroundings, pick a calming color—whatever color makes you feel the best or most relaxed. Furnish your environment with items that make you comfortable. Surround yourself with only the items that spark joy. Once you are relaxed and comfortable, healing can begin. Also, your safety is equally important, especially for healing of this kind. If you do not feel safe, your healing will be hindered. Which brings us to privacy.

INSIST ON YOUR PRIVACY

Privacy is paramount to the healing process. Safety and privacy go hand-in-hand. If you do not have privacy, you will not feel safe. You must insist that you have privacy when you are going through any kind of healing, especially emotional healing. Everyone has their own way of healing. What works for one person may not work for another. This kind of healing takes time—months, maybe even years. You do not have to share your emotional experience with anyone other than your counselor or therapist until you have sufficiently healed. You may decide never to talk to anyone about your sexual abuse other than counselors or therapists, and that is okay. We will talk about counseling and therapy in the next chapter. Privacy includes doctor-patient confidentiality, which we will also discuss in the next chapter. All of these things help build trust, which is especially important in the doctor-patient relationship. Always limit the number of people to whom you tell personal information. You would not want to be victimized again. I once told a close friend many things about my childhood, including how I was abused. She later breeched my confidence by telling someone else. This hurt me so deeply that we were never friends again.

SUMMARY

In this chapter, we learned about locating helpful resources such as choosing books on the subject of abuse and healing, removing bad influences, finding supportive people, creating a supportive environment, and insisting on your privacy. All of these are important steps to your healing process. If you put into practice what you have learned in this chapter, you will be ready for the next steps.

In the next chapter, you will learn how to choose between counseling or therapy. We will discuss whether medication can help or is necessary. We will also explore group therapy and time blocking for healing. These are all options you should consider. You must be certain that the therapist or counselor you choose is the right fit. Also, you must schedule time for these important considerations.

1. How did you feel when reading this chapter?

2. What new insights did you discover about yourself while working through this chapter?

3. What new discoveries about others and the world around you did you find?

4. What do you plan on doing next or doing differently in the future?

Chapter 3

Counseling or Therapy?

"You can do anything as long as you have the passion, the drive, the focus, and the support."

— Sabrina Bryan

In the last chapter, we learned about locating helpful resources such as choosing books on the subject of healing, removing bad influences, finding supportive people, avoiding abusive relationships, creating a supportive environment, and insisting on your privacy. All of these are important steps in your healing process. Once your environment is in place and your supportive people are found, you can really begin your healing process. You should be more relaxed by this point and able to understand what triggers your memories and emotions.

In this chapter, the real hard work will take place. We will explore the options for counseling or therapy, as well as group therapy. You will have the chance to decide which is right for you. We will look at meditation and the use of medications when they are necessary. We will also talk about the importance of time blocking for the healing process. These are important decisions to consider because your mental and emotional health depend on them. Take your time with each of these areas until you feel comfortable with your decisions.

COUNSELING

Have you ever wondered if the abuse you suffered really affected you on a personal or professional level? Maybe it affects the way you interact with people in general. Maybe you are shy at parties and social events. Counseling can be a particularly useful tool for your healing, especially if you do not know where to start. Of course, finding a suitable counselor is kind of like buying a car. Would you buy a car without test-driving it first? You want to try out a counselor before making a commitment. You want to know if they are the right fit. I tried at least four of them before deciding to work with one for a while. When choosing a counselor, you will want to find one who, first and foremost, believes you. They should never minimize what has happened to you. This person should have experience working with sexual abuse survivors. They should always keep their focus on you and not talk about or compare any of their personal experiences with yours. They should never push you to do anything you do not feel comfortable doing. Finally, they should never try to develop a friendship with you. That would be totally unethical. They should be encouraging you to build your support system by guiding you to the proper resources. Also, they should help you learn the skills you need to take care of yourself.

THERAPY

Choosing to go to therapy or a therapist can be pricey, but I highly recommend doing so if it's right for your situation. I eventually turned to a psychologist because the counselor I chose kept claiming to be a psychic, and she would often talk about her personal life, which I did not think was quite right. Once I found a psychologist, I realized how unethical she was. My therapist told me that therapists and counselors should never reveal their personal lives to patients. I found out just how wrong it was after talking with my therapist for a few sessions. Also, realize there is a difference between a psychologist and a psychiatrist. The psychiatrist can prescribe medications, whereas the psychologist cannot. Either way, I would think of it as a job interview for the counselor or therapist. Make sure the therapist is the right fit. You will want to know if you can trust this person and feel comfortable with them so you can open up to them about your deepest emotions. It can be scary to be that vulnerable with a stranger. Therapy can be very costly but can often be covered by insurance. Check with your provider. When I was in therapy, I really started to see a difference in my healing. My mindset was changing for the better. I stopped blaming myself for a lot of things. We will talk more about self-blame in the next chapter.

MEDITATION VS. MEDICATION

Are you worried all the time? Is it hard for you to fall asleep at times? Perhaps you have nightmares or experience flashbacks of your abuse. Do you feel like someone is out to get you all the time? If so, it may be time to consider medication. Medication does have its place in the healing process for some people, but not for all. I would consider medication only as a last resort. First, try meditation; guided meditation is a good place to start. It helps you focus your thoughts. According to the Chopra Center, “In meditation we disrupt the unconscious progression of thoughts and emotions by focusing on a new object of attention.”[2] You can find plenty of resources for meditation online. You could just find a quiet comfortable place in your home to relax and unwind from your day. Perhaps play some soft music if you must drown out any distracting noises. Some people use a fountain because they find the sound of running water to be soothing. You can also join a group for meditation; check out community events calendars or ask at health and wellness related centers, such as yoga centers. Meditation often relaxes the body as well as the mind as you refocus your attention.

For additional information on meditation, visit:

suzanneheyn.com/meditation-technique-emotional-healing/

chopra.com/articles/healing-the-source-of-emotional-pain

pushingbeauty.com/articles/meditation-healing-emotions

GROUP THERAPY

Group therapy is another form of talk therapy. It is usually recommended after one has been through individual therapy. Attending group therapy is somewhat similar to going to an AA meeting. Everyone is usually on a first-name basis there. It is considered a safe environment. Everything remains confidential. I tried it once, long before I was ready for it. Group therapy is not for everyone, and you should have a referral before you join a group. No judging is allowed in the group therapy process, and everyone gets a turn to speak, usually moderated by a counselor or therapist who knows everyone involved. I tried group therapy at the beginning of my process, but I quickly realized I was not ready for it. Later, I determined it was not something suited for me. However, I recommend you try it to decide for yourself.

TIME BLOCKING FOR HEALING

Blocking out some time each day for your healing process is particularly important. It is something you will want to work on every day. It is just as vital to your health as eating properly and exercising. Your emotional and mental health is just as important as your physical health. Just as you would schedule your exercise routine, you should schedule your healing routine. This may mean getting up earlier, before everyone else in your house, and having quiet time to read and work on yourself. To write this book, I had to block out time every day. It was not easy, but I decided I had to make a habit of it and schedule it into my day.

If you do not schedule time in your day for healing, you may start going backward in your healing process. Always keep going forward; do not look back. Dwelling on the past will not help you. Continuing with bad habits will not help you heal; we will talk more about habits in a later chapter.

As I wrote this book, I struggled with time blocking. If I did not schedule it into my day, into my to-do list, or whatever system I was using at the time, this book may never have been finished. To this day, I schedule everything, including visits with my friends. I keep a calendar on my phone where I can even set reminders.

SUMMARY

In this chapter, we explored the difference between counseling and therapy, and which is better for you and your specific needs. We also learned about meditation and medications; however, I prefer to stay away from meds. Group therapy is also an option, but usually after the initial therapy has ended. We even had a look at time blocking for your healing process. All these things are especially important and essential to the healing process. I am sure if you put these suggestions into practice, you will be well on your way to healing.

In the next chapter, we will talk about blame and where it really belongs. You will learn that being abused was not your fault so you should stop blaming yourself for what happened. You are worthy and you can create positive affirmations. You will also learn how celebrities overcame and healed from their sexual abuse experiences.

1. How did you feel when reading this chapter?

2. What new insights did you discover about yourself while working through this chapter?

3. What new discoveries about others and the world around you did you find?

4. What do you plan on doing next or doing differently in the future?

Chapter 4

Knowing It Is Not Your Fault

"The trust of the innocent is the liar's most useful tool."

—Stephen King

In the last chapter, we started the hard work of finding a counselor or therapist and considering group therapy. We also explored whether or not medications are necessary or if the technique of meditation may be helpful. Time blocking for the healing process is very important; make your healing process a regular part of your schedule.

In this chapter, you will learn why what happened to you was not your fault at all. You must learn to believe you are not to blame for what happened, and you *are* worthy of the life you have always wanted. We will explore using positive affirmations and learn a little about how some celebrities overcame their childhood sexual abuse. I hope some of these stories will inspire you to continue with your own healing. Perhaps you will, in turn, make a difference.

STOP BLAMING YOURSELF

Have you ever thought the abuse that happened to you was somehow your fault? That you did something to make your abuser think what they did to you was something you deserved? One of the most important things I want you to remember is: It was not your fault. Continuing to feel that way about yourself will only hurt your health. I want you to know and believe that what happened to you was never your fault.

Those who did this to you will want you to think it was your fault, but no, it was not. Please believe me when I tell you this. You are not to blame for anything that happened to you as a child. It was your parents' responsibility to keep you safe. Perhaps they were not even aware that you were being abused. Just keep telling yourself, "It is not my fault. I was only a child." Or you can say, "It is not my fault. I was the victim." We will explore self-talk in a later chapter.

THINKING YOU ARE WORTHY

It is important to your wellbeing that you believe you are worthy, worthy of healing, worthy of health, worthy of your own happiness. I used to think I was not worthy of the good things in life because of my past. Someone who blames themselves for the bad things that happen to them because of their past is misguided and stuck in their own thought patterns. We will discuss more about this in Chapter 15. It is imperative to believe you are worthy because it is true.

You have definite value as a human being. You may still have memories of things people said to you in the past that were not true. Those things may have been said to you out of someone else's anger or frustration. They may have been feeling bad about themselves and taken it out on you. It was their problem and not yours. Each person has their own unique talents they bring to the world; it is just a matter of finding yours.

Some victims think they are not worthy of love from another. They imagine they are damaged goods and not worth anyone's love. These are the same people who walk around with their heads down, not making any eye contact with anyone. So, I challenge you to walk around with your head up like you have all the confidence in the world. Someone once told me "Fake it until you make it." I think that is what you have to do. I used to think I was "damaged goods" until I got counseling and therapy.

POSITIVE AFFIRMATIONS

One way to help you change the way you think about yourself is to use positive affirmations. Instead of talking to yourself or about yourself negatively, try using some positive thoughts and saying things like, "I am worthy," "I am valued," "I am strong," "I can do it," etc. Put those affirmations on paper and hang them on a wall where you can see them daily. Many successful people do this. Someone once told me "What you think about, you bring about." There is power in positive thinking. If you focus on creating positive changes in your life, they will happen. Have you ever heard it said that some people see a glass as half-full or half-empty? That is the difference between a positive and a negative thinker. A positive thinker sees the glass as half-full, whereas a negative thinker will see it as half-empty. Either way, the glass itself is the same; it's the perception that is different. If you have a negative perception of the world, chances are you received negative messages from people during your formative years. When you were growing up, you may have encountered messages from people you trusted who were not so nice. Perhaps they were telling you that you were worthless, no good, or would never make anything of yourself. You can change this negative self-talk into positive self-talk. Yes, you can. It requires being very mindful of your thoughts throughout the day and consciously changing each negative into a positive. This change may take some considerable effort just like it does when you need to change any habit. When you catch yourself thinking a negative thought, immediately replace it with a positive one. For example, you are about to take a tiny step out of your comfort zone when you think to yourself, "I can't do this!" Stop! Say to yourself, "This is the only way I can grow as a person!" Try it; it works!

HOW CELEBRITIES OVERCAME

"Nearly half the nation's children have experienced at least one or more traumatic events, including physical or sexual abuse, or neglect," according to Linda Rosenberg on thenationalcouncil.org. To help a survivor overcome their abuse, we must be compassionate. We must ask them what happened to them and believe them when they tell us. They are more likely to open up if they feel they are believed. In my research, I learned that Oprah Winfrey was an abuse victim as a child. However, she found a way to overcome it. In an interview, she said, "My father turned my life around by insisting that I be more than I was. His love of learning showed me the way." Oprah's father insisted she get an education. She took drama and public speaking at Nashville East High School and even became class president. Today, she is a proponent of positive thinking. Her unique life experiences helped her gain a certain empathy for other people. She took advantage of opportunities that propelled her to success. For instance, she won a public speaking contest, which led her to a full scholarship to Tennessee State University.[3]

Singer Mary J. Blige was raped by a family friend. "I remember feeling, literally right before it happened, I just could not believe that this person was going to do this to me," Blige said. "That thing followed me all my life. The shame of thinking my molestation was my fault—it led me to believe I wasn't worth anything." Later, Blige took all that pain and poured it into her songs.

As an eight-year-old, Chris Brown was having sex with a fourteen- or fifteen-year-old from the neighborhood. Although this behavior was "consensual, from a legal standpoint it was considered rape, even if she was under 18 years old," explains Iva Anthony of the online publication

Madame Noire.[4] In addition, Ashley Judd used her memoirs of abuse as her therapy and to help other abused women with their healing process.[5]

In an interview with TV host Ellen DeGeneres, actress Busy Phillips talked about her book, *This Will Only Hurt a Little*, in which she talks about being raped at age fourteen.[6] Phillips encourages other victims to speak out and share their experiences. DeGeneres herself was raped at age fifteen.[7] When asked "Why did you wait so long to talk about it?" DeGeneres replied, "As girls, we were taught not to say anything, and we are taught to just go along with it." DeGeneres and Phillips struggled for so long with being victims that they recommend we teach our children to speak up.

In her book, *The Life of a Wannabe Mogul*, Bella Thorne writes poetry about her experiences with sexual abuse and depression. In school, she was bullied for her dyslexia. She felt pressured to be sexy. She was abused from the age of six to adolescence. Since she grew up with the abuse, she felt it was "normal." In a recent interview, Thorne says she struggles with self-acceptance and she spoke about Stockholm syndrome.[8] Wikipedia states:

> **Stockholm syndrome** has been defined as a condition in which hostages develop a psychological alliance with their captors during captivity. Emotional bonds may be formed between captor and captives, during intimate time together, but these are generally considered irrational considering the danger or risk endured by the victims.[9]

Dancing with the Stars celebrity Cheryl Burke felt some relief after writing her book, *Dancing Lessons*, in which she talks about the abuse she experienced. She says she is still in the process of healing herself. She was molested by a man who was entrusted to watch her. She says he was the father figure she was looking for. He sensed she had a need and he tried to fill it. He would cuddle her and tell her he loved her. He would have her watch pornographic movies, but he never hurt her physically. At her tender young age, she did not realize what he was doing was wrong, and she was too scared to speak out. He was not caught until another girl, whom he tried to molest, stopped him and spoke out to her mother. Cheryl ended up testifying against him in court at age six. At the time, she felt guilty and confused. After that, she grew up with no self-esteem, had some abusive relationships, and struggled with boundary issues. She said she had "no self-respect for who I am."[10]

Pamela Anderson, the star of TV's *Baywatch*, said she was often embarrassed about her abuse and would blame herself for what had happened. "I learned to never put myself in that situation again," Anderson says. She even had her own encounter with Harvey Weinstein where she refused him, after which he went off on her verbally. Now she speaks out about pornographic addiction. She also admits that she has taken advantage of her sensuality.[11]

SUMMARY

In this chapter, you learned that what happened to you was not your fault and you should not blame yourself for it.

You must continue to understand that you are worthy of a normal life. You can and will have what you want if you understand it is possible even for you. We also learned in this chapter about positive affirmations and how they can help you achieve your goals. Finally, you learned about celebrities who have suffered sexual abuse and how they have overcame their challenges.

In the next chapter, we will embrace our inner child by thinking about what we would tell them to encourage them to be strong and stand up for themselves. We will talk about how to feed your soul or spirituality, whether you be Christian, Jewish, Muslim, Hindu, Buddhist, or have some other belief system. Perhaps feeding your soul is just a matter of doing something outdoors. Then we will talk about letting go of shame, especially since we already discussed that it was not your fault in the previous chapter. Finally, we will touch upon the grieving process—grieving for one's lost innocence at such a young age.

1. How did you feel when reading this chapter?

2. What new insights did you discover about yourself while working through this chapter?

3. What new discoveries about others and the world around you did you find?

4. What do you plan on doing next or doing differently in the future?

Chapter 5

Embracing Your Inner Child

"Hold the hand of the child that lives in your soul. For this child, nothing is impossible."

—Paulo Coelho, Author

In the last chapter, you learned that what happened to you was not your fault and you should not blame yourself for it. If I sound like I am repeating myself, it is because I am. I want you to continue to understand and believe you are worthy of a normal and successful life. You can and will have what you want if you understand and believe it is possible even for you. We also learned about positive affirmations and how they can help you achieve your goals. Most importantly, you learned which celebrities suffered sexual abuse and how they overcame their challenges. Their stories can serve as inspiration for you to persevere.

In this chapter, we will explore the idea of reclaiming your inner child. You will find ways in which to feed your soul, whether it is through a belief in a Higher Power, like God, Buddha, or Allah, or whatever you believe in. Perhaps just being in the great outdoors feeds your soul. We will also work on letting go of shame and the grieving process. These things are all important steps in your healing process.

THINGS YOU WOULD TELL YOUR YOUNGER SELF

Have you ever wished you could live your childhood over again and be a parent to yourself? Well, you can, in a way. In his book *Homecoming: Reclaiming and Healing Your Inner Child*, John Bradshaw explains it well. I highly recommend reading it or any of Bradshaw's other books. You can do it for yourself. It is possible to reclaim and champion your inner child. Karl Melvin of http://toxicescape.com writes about Bradshaw's books, "Broken into 4 stages, the books cover key developmental phases (such as Toddler, Pre-school and school age), the negative experiences that might have influenced the natural evolution of this phase and how to heal the subsequent wounds, so they no longer impact your adult life."

FEED YOUR SOUL

Do you believe in a Higher Power? God, as it were? I am a Christian. That is, I believe Christ died for my sins. Knowing this gives me hope for the future. Find your God or Higher Power and let Him take the burden from you. If you do not belong to a church, I recommend you find one. First, it is a great place to find new friends. However, you may want to take your time and find the right church, one that makes you feel comfortable. This may take a while. When I was looking for a new church, I tried a few before I settled on one in my neighborhood. Once you have decided on a church, make sure you get involved in some small group activity like a Bible study or volunteering. Joining small groups are one way to make new friends and find supportive people who may help you in your healing process.

Another way to feed your soul is to do things that rejuvenate you. Personally, I love to work in my vegetable and flower gardens. There is something therapeutic about manual labor and working with your hands in the soil. I feel it is important to balance your mental and emotional healing with some physical exercise, whatever kind works for you. You may like to walk on the beach, hike in the woods, or go sailing, biking, or kayaking. Perhaps you have a dog and like to go jogging with him. This may be the time to revisit an old hobby or take up a new one.

Do not forget, the healing process can get overwhelming. If you start to feel overwhelmed, stop for a moment to think about what may have caused it. Sometimes, you may have taken on too much. You may have to say "no" to some things to have time for your healing. Do not feel bad about this; your healing is vitally important and should be taken seriously. Remember the process of time blocking in Chapter 3?

If you start to feel overwhelmed, you may have to stop for a while and relax. It may be helpful to turn off for a while and take a break from your hard work. Take the time to recharge your brain. Perhaps do something fun or physical. Try something that does not require a lot of brain power. Pretty soon you will feel refreshed and ready to get back to your healing work.

LETTING GO OF SHAME

"You'll never be free until you let go of the things that weigh you down."

— Anonymous

In Chapter 4, we talked about the fact that what happened to you was not your fault and that you are worthy of healing. So, now is the time to let go of shame. You have no reason to feel shame. As I have said before, what happened to you was someone else's fault and you are not to be blamed. It is time for your healing process to begin (or continue). If you were a child at the time of your abuse, there is no reason for shame on your part. Your perpetrator, however, should feel shame for hurting you. You have nothing to be ashamed about. Carrying shame around for years does you no good and can cause you illness. Let it go!

Remember Angie's story in Chapter 1? She told me when she was kidnapped that "You do anything to save your life" and "You will say anything to save your life." These are the things that later bring on shame. She also told me she "felt dirty and didn't want to be touched." Basically, she and I were "shamed into silence," as she put it. My shame kept me from having many friends. I was always afraid of getting hurt or having my past be found out.

GRIEVING

As a child, if we lose a pet, we grieve for it. We feel sad and lonely for a while, but we usually get over it rather quickly. How long does it take for someone to grieve over the loss of their innocence, especially if it was lost at a young age? I believe the time is different for everyone. It could take years, even decades. On grief.com, David Kessler writes, "When inappropriate sexual behavior first happens, there is the loss of safety and innocence. There is deep fear of standing up to those who hold the key to our career and success. Violation replaces the golden rule. And in grief, secrecy becomes shame." I believe we must go through some sort of grieving process to let go of the shame.

Once someone realizes how much of their innocence was lost, they often cry just as though they were grieving for a lost loved one. They realize their childhood was robbed of its safety. The length of the grieving process is different for everyone.

Read more at: grief.com/sexual-harassment-assault-grief/

SUMMARY

In this chapter, we explored the idea of reclaiming your inner child. You found ways to feed your soul, whether it was through belief in a Higher Power, like God, Buddha, Allah, or whatever Supreme Being or Source you believe in. It could have been just being in the great outdoors. We also worked on letting go of shame and the grieving process. These things are all important steps in your healing process. We must grieve before we can move on.

In the next chapter, we will work on learning to be comfortable with yourself and being your own best friend. We will work on changing your self-talk—the things you tell yourself about yourself. We will also work on not being judgmental because not all people are the same. Just because one person abused you doesn't mean the next person you meet will. And finally, we will help you find ways to embrace your uniqueness.

1. How did you feel when reading this chapter?

2. What new insights did you discover about yourself while working through this chapter?

3. What new discoveries about others and the world around you did you find?

4. What do you plan on doing next or doing differently in the future?

Chapter 6

Being Comfortable With Yourself

"Knowing yourself is the beginning of all wisdom."

— Aristotle

In the last chapter, we explored the idea of reclaiming your inner child. You found ways to feed your soul, including through a belief in a Higher Power, like God, Buddha, Allah, or whatever Supreme Being or Source you believe in. Perhaps you feed your soul just by being in the great outdoors. We also worked on letting go of shame and the grieving process. These things are all important steps in your healing process. Grieving is fundamental to the healing process.

In this chapter, we will work on being comfortable with yourself, being your own best friend. We will work on changing your self-talk, the things you tell yourself about yourself. Now is the time to start thinking positively. We will also work on not being judgmental because not all people are the same. There are plenty of good people to go around; it is just a matter of finding them. And finally, we will help you find ways to embrace your uniqueness, which is what makes you what you are.

BECOMING YOUR OWN BEST FRIEND

Have you ever heard anyone say, "If you can't love yourself, then how do you expect anyone else to love you?" I really do not know who said it, but I remember hearing it. When you are comfortable with yourself, it really shows. Confidence shows on your face. A confident person will look you in the eye when they speak to you. I know if you are at the beginning of your healing process, loving yourself or feeling confident can seem difficult. It took me a long time before I felt comfortable with myself. I used to look to others for approval to boost my self-esteem. I used to think if everyone liked me, then I was a likeable person and had value. If no one liked me, well, then I was not anybody. This is no way to think about yourself. Everyone has value. It is a matter of accepting yourself for who you are and your unique talents. Everyone has talents of some sort or another. Some have discovered theirs; others have yet to find theirs. It really does not matter what other people think of you anyway.

I wasted decades of my life wallowing in self-pity, believing I did not deserve any more than what I already had. My beliefs were self-limiting, and I was not convinced I could do any better or be any better. Only after I went through counseling and therapy did I realize my true potential. To this day, I am still realizing it. Yes, one's true potential is limitless. You are only limited by what you think you can do. Anything you put your mind to you can do or achieve.

CHANGE YOUR SELF-TALK

Have you ever said something to yourself like, "I'm so stupid!" or "I can't do anything right"? You might have said something like that after making a mistake. This is called negative self-talk. You need to stop it now! It does you no good. It only perpetuates sadness and depression. It is important that you replace every negative thought with a positive one. Instead, say something like, "I am not stupid. I can learn from this mistake." On his website, Nick Wignall says, "events themselves do not cause us suffering, it's the way we think about events that influences how we feel. And thanks to some good science over the past 50 years or so, we've basically confirmed this and solidified it in what's known as Cognitive Mediation Theory."[12]

I believe it was my therapist who first suggested I consciously make note of what I said to myself, when, and why. At first, I just kept track of how often I had negative thoughts and what triggered them. Next, I tried to substitute some more positive language. I literally said to myself, "This is not me. I can do better!" Here is what you must do: Every time you find yourself thinking negatively, stop and think about it for a minute. Where did that thought come from? What do you think caused it? What can you do to stop it or change it to something positive? Success coach and author Hal Elrod said, "The moment you take responsibility for everything in your life is the moment you can change anything in your life."

I used to play music whenever I drove my car, mostly to drown out the voices in my head. Do not get me wrong. I was not really hearing voices; it was just my negative self-talk. I would do some of the same things at home with the TV. I would turn it on just to have background noise. Now, I am happy to say I do not need to drive with the radio on, and I do not always have the TV on in my house either. As a matter of fact, my radio is broken in my car now so I enjoy the silence! So, it can be done, my negative self-talk has mostly been changed. As with any new habit, it all takes time to establish. We will talk more about habits in Chapter 10.

In some of the lines below, list some of the negative self-talk you might have been using. In the rest of the lines, list some positive self-talk you can use to replace the negative.

STOP JUDGING; ALL PEOPLE ARE NOT THE SAME

"Do not judge, or you will be judged."

— Matthew 7:1

Have you ever seen someone and assumed something negative about them just from their looks? What if someone thought that way about you? Do not judge anyone unless you have walked a mile in their shoes. If we are Christians, we are supposed to abide by this verse above from Matthew; however, many fail miserably at it—myself included. I found out I was wrongly passing judgment while at a church function. I was observing a man who appeared a bit unkempt and dirty and sounded like he was talking to himself. In reality, he was publicly commenting on what the pastor was saying. Turns out the gentleman I was judging internally is a veteran. I felt a little embarrassed, but fortunately, only because of my own thoughts. So, in retrospect, one shouldn't judge others, especially for the way they look. You don't know their back stories and shouldn't assume they are abusers based on appearance or first impressions.

Do not give up on love. Don't assume everyone will mistreat you. There is still a chance you can find someone who adores you. There are good people out there; it is just a matter of finding them. However, if you have not finished your healing process, you should not be looking for love yet. Besides, when the timing and the person are right, love will find you. I was truly fortunate enough to find the love of my life early on. He respects me and loves me for who I am. We have grown together in our love and created a wonderful family. You can certainly have the same for your life.

EMBRACING YOUR UNIQUENESS

Each of us is unique. No two snowflakes are alike. No two fingerprints are alike either, not even for identical twins. If we were all the same, this world would be very boring. Therefore, I say, "Embrace your uniqueness!" God made you the way you are for a reason, so rejoice and be glad in it! We all add value to the world in unique ways. Each of us has talents we can contribute. As teenagers, we try so hard to fit in with the crowd. Then, we try to set ourselves apart for that job interview. Sometimes our lives send us from one extreme to another; just do not lose yourself in the process. That which makes you unique and special is important.

Perhaps you have not found your talent. Do not worry; someday it will come to you. Grandma Moses did not start painting until she was seventy-eight. Do not give up on yourself. Everyone can find their passion and succeed.

SUMMARY

In this chapter, we worked on learning to be comfortable with ourselves and being our own best friend. We worked on changing our self-talk—the things we tell ourselves about ourselves. Now is the time to start thinking positive thoughts. We also worked on not being judgmental of others. Remember that not all men and not all women are bad. Finally, we helped find ways for you to embrace your uniqueness—it is what makes you who you are.

In the next chapter, we will focus on releasing emotions. There are healthy and unhealthy ways to release your emotions. It is important for you to know the difference for your health and safety, not to mention the health and safety of those around you. Releasing your emotions, however, is better than stuffing them. We will also talk about drug and alcohol abuse because many victims of sexual abuse turn to these vices to mask their pain and/or suppress their emotions. Doing so only makes things worse or prolongs the healing process.

1. How did you feel when reading this chapter?

2. What new insights did you discover about yourself while working through this chapter?

3. What new discoveries about others and the world around you did you find?

4. What do you plan on doing next or doing differently in the future?

Chapter 7

Releasing Emotions

"Feel the feeling but don't become the emotion. Witness it. Allow it. Release it."

— Crystal Andrus

In the last chapter, we worked on being comfortable with ourselves, on being our own best friend. We worked on changing our self-talk, the things we tell ourselves about ourselves. Now is the time to start thinking positive thoughts. We also worked on not being judgmental. And finally, we talked about the need to embrace your uniqueness. It is what makes you who you are.

In this chapter, we will focus on releasing emotions. There are healthy and unhealthy ways to release your emotions. It is important for you to know the difference, for your health and safety, not to mention the health and safety of those around you. Releasing your emotions, when done in healthy ways, is better than stuffing them. We will also talk about drug and alcohol abuse because many victims turn to these vices to mask their pain and/or suppress their emotions. This behavior only makes things worse or prolongs the healing process.

UNHEALTHY WAYS VS. HEALTHY WAYS

Have you ever felt so mad or frustrated that you wanted to hit someone or something? I am sure we all have been there at one point or another. Children have temper tantrums; some adults do too. You have seen on TV when an umpire and a coach disagree; they are face to face, yelling at each other and kicking sand. Or how about when a tennis player throws their racket? Yes, even adults have temper tantrums. Some of these tantrums can be unhealthy behaviors that are not helpful in your healing process. Screaming, yelling, and breaking things just because you are mad or upset about anything is not healthy behavior; it only hurts the ones around you. If you have children, this behavior is not setting a good example for them on how to handle their emotions. Try to find a healthier way to release your emotions, like screaming into a pillow, tearing up old newspapers, crushing aluminum cans, or pulling weeds. When I get angry and frustrated, I sometimes go on a cleaning frenzy. Once I was so mad at my sister-in-law that I dug post holes for an entire horse corral. So, the next time you find yourself getting angry and worked up over something or someone, try raking leaves, vacuuming the floor, or washing your car instead of flying off the handle, breaking things, or yelling at someone. You will feel better about yourself, and your family will be happier about it too! If you must, release your emotions during a therapy session. Your therapist may offer you suggestions for healthy ways to release your emotions.

Let us return to Angie's story. At one point, Angie tried and failed to commit suicide. She also had a friend commit suicide. Then she had a three-year breakdown, during which she tried self-mutilation, but she also began to read the Bible. Reading the Bible was one of the good things she did. Angie says, "You don't have to stay broke." She used the Bible as a guidebook for her healing, referring back to it frequently for advice. Her Bible was a friend to her, helping her to focus and find clarity.

DON'T STUFF YOUR EMOTIONS

Stuffing your emotions is not healthy. Keeping them bottled up inside you can cause health problems that will eventually show up in one form or another, ranging anywhere from digestive issues to a full-on nervous breakdown. Eventually, you may just explode with all that emotion and not know what to do with it. Find something you like to do as a way to express your emotions, such as music or art therapy. I will discuss these more in Chapter 12. If you are angry, sign up for a kickboxing class and take it out on a punching bag. Who knows? You may even get into great shape in the process. If that is not your style, try running, chopping wood, or even digging holes for fence posts. Do not laugh; as I said earlier, digging holes was what I once did with my anger.

My point is: Do something more constructive with your anger and frustration. Perhaps you will even come up with a creative solution for whatever is frustrating you.

ALCOHOL AND DRUG ABUSE

This is an especially important subject. Have you ever tried to stuff your emotion and pain by taking drugs or alcohol? Many people have, and many people have lost their lives doing it. Many people get stuck in addiction because they do not deal with their emotional and mental health. I have tried not to deal with it myself, and let me tell you, it does you no good whatsoever. Please believe me, I have made a ton of mistakes. I have drank so much that I have made myself sick and have forgotten by the next day what I did or said while I was drunk. I have even been arrested for drunk driving. That was a real eye-opener and a pivotal moment in my life. I spent time in jail. Let me tell you, there were some scary characters in there. Even though I only spent two days in there, I *seriously* would not want to do it again or wish it on anyone else.

If you have a problem or even think you may have a problem with drugs or alcohol, you should seek treatment. Drug and alcohol treatment is often covered by health insurance, so check with your provider. Many people have great success from joining a local AA (Alcoholics Anonymous) group. Other similar groups include Narcotics Anonymous, Gamblers Anonymous, and Overeaters Anonymous, plus probably a few I do not even know about. Each group helps people overcome their addictions. There is usually a Twelve-Step process for healing within these groups. You will be paired up with a "sponsor," someone who has been through the process themselves, who will be your guide, lifeline, and support person.

SUMMARY

In this chapter, we worked on releasing emotions. There are healthy and unhealthy ways to release your emotions. It is important for you to know the difference, for your health and safety, plus the health and safety of those around you. Releasing your emotions, in healthy ways, is always better than stuffing them. We also talked about drug and alcohol abuse and how many victims turn to these vices to mask their pain or suppress their emotions. We learned that this behavior only makes things worse or prolongs the healing process.

In the next chapter, we will discuss forgiving your transgressors, as well as confronting your abusers. I know that sounds weird, but the process is more for you than for them. I will explain this process more in the next chapter. You must be prepared for anything during this confrontation. Once it is over, you may want to seek some spirituality. The next chapter will be intense, so I want you to be prepared for that.

1. How did you feel when reading this chapter?

2. What new insights did you discover about yourself while working through this chapter?

3. What new discoveries about others and the world around you did you find?

4. What do you plan on doing next or doing differently in the future?

Chapter 8

Forgiving Your Transgressors

"Forgive others not because they deserve forgiveness, but because you deserve peace."

— Anonymous

In the last chapter, we worked on releasing emotions. It is better to release your emotions than stuff them. However, there are healthy and unhealthy ways to release your emotions. It is important for you to know the difference, for your health and safety and the health and safety of others around you. We also talked about drug and alcohol abuse and how many victims turn to these vices to mask their pain and/or suppress their emotions. We learned that such behavior only makes things worse or prolongs the healing process.

In this chapter, we will discuss forgiving your transgressors as well as confronting your abusers. As I said before, this process is more for you than for them. This will be a difficult chapter. You must be prepared for anything during the confrontation. Once it is over, you may want to seek some spirituality. You have come this far in this book, which tells me you are serious about your healing. Do not give up now! In the beginning of my healing process, I never thought I would confront anyone.

CONFRONTING THE ABUSER

Have you ever wanted to confront your abuser to tell them how you felt during the time you were abused? Have you ever wanted to yell at them to tell them what a creep you really think they are? Have you ever wanted to publicly humiliate or shame them for what they did to you? I know I always wanted to publicly humiliate the creeps who abused and took advantage of me. However, I spoke about this subject with my therapist long before I had any confrontation. Furthermore, I was unable to track down all my abusers. That can happen when it takes decades to figure out what really happened to you and how to heal from it.

Confrontations are complicated and scary. You must consider many things before going through with one. How are you going to feel before, during, and after the confrontation? You may want to practice by doing some role-playing with your therapist or counselor or with a good friend you trust. This can be a very scary process. You do not know how your abuser will react. Some abusers may be totally oblivious to how you were affected by the abuse. Others may think you are totally overreacting and will minimize your emotions.

BEING PREPARED

If your abuser is a family member, be aware that the confrontation may be met with such adverse reactions that it completely divides your family. It happened to me even though the abuser was not a family member but close family friend; part of my family took my abuser's side while other family members supported me and the truth. Fortunately, my parents believed me and supported me in my healing process. However, I want you to be prepared to be ostracized from your family if they do not agree with you about what the perpetrator did. Things could get messy. It did for me in the beginning. After a while, things started to cool down and the family, including the close friend who had abused me, began to reconcile. I also want you to be prepared for this process to take an exceptionally long time, or perhaps never be resolved. For me, it took a good ten years before things started to settle. Even now, the healing process for my family is still going on after fifteen years. It is entirely possible that you may not be able to reconcile at all. In that case, you will be far better off just staying away from those who do not support you. Your health and wellbeing are what is most important while you are still healing.

Prepare yourself for feeling revictimized by your family members, especially if the perpetrator denies or minimizes the truth, or worse yet, blames you for whatever reason. According to Miranda Pacchiana, a survivor, there are seven ways that family members revictimize sexual abuse survivors.[13] After denying, minimizing, and blaming the survivor, family members may just tell the survivor to move on with their life. When my perpetrator tried blaming me, thankfully my parents believed me. Some family members may refuse to listen to the victims, while others may just refuse to take sides; neither of these responses is supportive. "Some families leave survivors out of family events and social gatherings, even while their abusers are included," says Pacchiana.

SEEKING SPIRITUALITY

I talked about feeding your soul in Chapter 5 and touched on relying on a Higher Power. Most people believe in a Higher Power. You may call this Higher Power God, Allah, Mother Earth, or another name. I am a Christian, but even I had to change churches until I found one where I felt at home. A church family can be extremely helpful in your healing journey. Church is a great place to make new friends and find useful resources. Some churches can even help you with some living expenses on a month-by-month basis, with limitations. Spirituality is different for each person. In an interview with David Letterman, Oprah Winfrey, after her sexual abuse experience, said, "I really did believe there was a power greater than myself." She added that there was nothing in her life she would ever take back. "Everybody has a story, and your story is equally as valuable and important as my story. My story just helped define and shape me as does everybody's story."[14] Becoming spiritual and learning to rely on your Higher Power is something you may want to work on before or after the confrontation process.

SUMMARY

In this chapter, we discussed forgiving your transgressors and confronting your abusers. This process is more to help you than them. This was a difficult chapter. You must be prepared for anything during the confrontation. Before or after, you may want to seek some spirituality. Now you are about halfway through this book; that tells me you are serious about your healing. Do not give up now! In the beginning of my healing process, I never thought I would be able to confront anyone, but I did.

In the next chapter, we will discuss moving on with life. I honestly believe you should start slowly, as with any healing process. We will be working on making new friends, which is hard enough on its own, let alone when you are healing from sexual abuse. Next, we will prioritize your needs, which include nourishing your body. Having a healthy body helps the emotional healing process.

1. How did you feel when reading this chapter?

2. What new insights did you discover about yourself while working through this chapter?

3. What new discoveries about others and the world around you did you find?

4. What do you plan on doing next or doing differently in the future?

Chapter 9

Moving On With Life

"Life is like riding a bicycle. To keep your balance, you must keep moving."

— Albert Einstein

In the last chapter, we discussed forgiving your transgressors and confronting your abusers. This process is more for you than for them. You learned that you must be prepared for anything during this confrontation. Before or after the confrontation is over, you may want to seek some spirituality. I am proud of you for making so much progress so far; it shows me that you are serious about healing. Do not give up now! Keep moving forward; you will make it, and do not be afraid of the confrontation. Believe me, you will feel better afterward for being brave enough to do it.

In this chapter, we will work on moving on with life. I genuinely believe you should start slow, as with any healing process. We will work on making new friends, which is hard enough in itself, let alone when you are healing from sexual abuse. Next, we will prioritize your needs, which include nourishing your body. Having a healthy body helps the emotional healing process.

START SLOW

Have you ever wanted to make a big change in your life and you jumped in with both feet, all gung-ho and everything, only to become overwhelmed and quit after two weeks or so? People starting a new exercise routine or dieters often do this. You want to know why? Well, I will tell you. It is because they did not start slow. Trying to make big changes too fast is a mistake many people make. Even AA people have a Twelve-Step program because it takes a long time to change your way of thinking, your mindset. Think of it as like learning a new language. First, start with the basic things in your life. Make sure you have a safe place to stay, clothes to wear, and food to eat. It does not have to be fancy, but it should be clean and something you can afford. If you must live with a trusted relative or friend until you get better arrangements, then so be it. Make slow, incremental changes that you can stick with until they become habits. First, a change in living arrangements. Next, a new job; then finally, new relationships, starting with friends.

Create a vision board. What is this? It is a board or canvas to visually display the things you want to be, do, or have in the future. I have made one myself. On my vision board, I put photos that I cut out of magazines to represent the things I wanted out of life. On this vision board, I placed photos of Hawaii because I wanted to go there on vacation. Within a year of creating that board, my husband and I went to Kauai, Hawaii, for a vacation! I also added new flooring—that came true! My point is: If you believe hard enough and work toward it, you can achieve anything you want.

MAKING NEW FRIENDS

Have you ever thought you needed new friends? Yes, I asked this question before. I once heard that you are the sum total of the five people you hang out with the most. Take a good, hard look at your friends. Do they care about you? Or are they using you for their own gain? Do your friends uplift you and make you feel good about yourself? Or are they self-centered and egotistical and make you feel small? Perhaps it is time to revisit the list you started in Chapter 2 of supportive and non-supportive people in your life. We are not meant to live in isolation. We need other people in our lives. Yes, I realize other people may have hurt you to the point that you do not want anything to do with them. Just remember this: Not everyone is out to hurt you. There are good people out there; it is just a matter of finding them. If you have found a church to join, get involved. Join a Bible study or small group. Find a Facebook group that is full of people who enjoy some of the same things you enjoy. I am a small business owner, so I joined a Facebook networking group. In this group, I gained many new friends who are also business owners. Through this group, I found a publishing coach who gave me the confidence to write this book and led me to the resources I needed to get it published.

PRIORITIZE YOUR NEEDS

Since you are moving on with your life, you may be moving on to a new home, possibly a totally new neighborhood. This also may be the first time you have lived on your own. You must prioritize your needs. First and foremost, where are you going to live? How are you going to pay for that? You may first have to live with friends or relatives you trust and then move on from there. You may also need to get an education, such as a GED or AA degree from your local community college. If you are truly on your own, you may qualify for scholarships. Stop in at your local community college's counseling department and ask to talk to someone about scholarships. I was told by my counselor to search for scholarships; she even told me where to start. Usually, there is an orientation class you will be recommended to take. This class usually has information on scholarships and other resources. An education is extremely helpful and useful. Most of the best jobs and all the higher-paying jobs require some sort of higher education like a bachelor's or master's degree.

NOURISH YOUR BODY

Have you ever felt run down, low on energy, or unable to concentrate? Me too. It usually means you have not been eating right. Nutritious food is essential to your wellbeing. I sure can tell the difference when I make healthier food choices. I am not a doctor, so I advise you to consult your doctor before making any radical changes to your diet. One thing I do know is you must have the right ratio of protein to carbohydrates at every meal. Make sure they are complex carbohydrates. This will help keep your blood sugars level for most of the day, especially if you eat regularly throughout the day. A healthy and nourished body has a better chance of having a healthy mind and emotions. Eating healthy foods will help regulate your hormones and control your weight.

First, start out by cutting out fast food and most processed foods. These are usually too high in fats, preservatives, salt, and sugars. Cut out all sugary drinks, including juices. They add unnecessary calories. Drink lots of water. Make sure you eat breakfast. They say it is the most important meal of the day. Exercise is just as important as diet. When I say diet, I do not mean trying to lose weight. I mean a diet for optimal health. Good health also includes regular exercise, which strengthens your heart, lungs, and muscles. Make sure some of your exercise includes weight bearing to strengthen your bones. Most doctors recommend you do thirty minutes of some type of exercise that will increase your heartrate every day. It can be something as simple as walking. So, grab a friend or your dog and start walking. Make this activity a daily habit; even schedule it into your day.

SUMMARY

In this chapter, we worked on moving on with life. I honestly believe you should start slowly, as with any healing process. Never put any more stress on yourself than is necessary. We also worked on making new friends. Then, we prioritized your needs, including nourishing your body. Emotional healing work requires a healthy body. Exercise is just as important as diet.

In the next chapter, we will discuss coping with change. When making lasting changes, start with the small stuff. We will work on forming good and healthy habits and explore ways to help you move on to become a better you. You will become your habits by choice because you will see positive changes in your life. Finally, we will discuss focusing on what you wish to become. You have control over your own destiny. It all starts with what you want out of life. It depends on how badly you want it.

1. How did you feel when reading this chapter?

2. What new insights did you discover about yourself while working through this chapter?

3. What new discoveries about others and the world around you did you find?

4. What do you plan on doing next or doing differently in the future?

Chapter 10

Coping With Change

"Change is the law of life. And those who look only to the past or present are certain to miss the future."

—John F. Kennedy

In the last chapter, we worked on moving on with life. Please remember it is best to start slowly, as with any healing process. Never put more stress on yourself than is necessary. We also worked on making new friends, which can be hard when healing from sexual abuse. Then, we prioritized your needs, which included nourishing your body and exercising. Emotional healing work requires a healthy body.

In this chapter, we will discuss coping with change. When making any lasting changes, you will want to start with the small stuff. We will work on forming good and healthy habits that will help you move on to become a better you. You will become your habits by choice because you will see positive changes in your life. Finally, we will discuss focusing on what you wish to become. I said it before and I will say it again, you have control over your own destiny. It all starts with what you want out of life. It depends on how badly you want it. How hard are you willing to work for that positive change?

START SMALL

Now that you have decided to move on with your life, what will you do next? Do you have a plan? Let's say you have moved into a new place in a new neighborhood. The next move should be to get to know your neighbors. This effort may be very scary and way out of your comfort zone, but it is necessary. You will want to know who your neighbors are, especially if you live in an apartment. That way, you know who belongs and who does not. You do not have to throw a party and invite the whole building. Just get to know one neighbor at a time; take them to lunch or coffee. Take the time to get to know them. Eventually, invite them to your home. Or if it makes you feel more comfortable, join a local church and make some new friends there.

To begin making positive changes, find a notebook and start writing down your specific goals. Categorize them as personal, financial, spiritual, and career goals or use whatever titles make sense to you. Next, prioritize these goals by importance. Personal and financial goals should probably be your most important ones; the rest will happen organically. In other words, the first two will help you get to the next two. Again, keep these steps small and manageable. In the space below, list some of your goals and a deadline for achieving them.

FORMING GOOD/HEALTHY HABITS

Have you ever thought that your habits might be what are holding you back from your potential? From your eating habits to your work habits, certain habits could be holding you back from your dreams. I had a bad habit of eating sugary snacks in the afternoon. Finally, I noticed that when I ate those snacks, they would make me sleepy after the sugar rush. Then I would be lazy and unproductive. Eventually, I realized I was getting nothing done in the afternoons.

First, make a list of the habits that you think might be holding you back. Then make a list of healthy habits you might use to replace the unhealthy ones. Instead of eating sugary snacks, I started doing some sort of activity that kept my mind and hands busy. If I were truly hungry, I would choose fruits or vegetables to snack on. I finally lost the last ten pounds I was hoping to lose and stayed much more alert in the afternoons.

I recommend reading the book *Atomic Habits* by James Clear. It provides some good examples and information on how to break bad habits and form new ones. Forming good habits will take time. In fact, James Clear says it takes approximately sixty-six days to form a new habit. It took a long time for you to form bad habits, so it will take equally as long for you to form good ones. However, if you follow the advice in this book and in the other books I suggest, you will succeed.

In the space below, make a list of all your unhealthy habits in the first column. Then, make a list of healthier habits in the second column to replace each of the unhealthy ones.

______________________	______________________
______________________	______________________
______________________	______________________
______________________	______________________
______________________	______________________
______________________	______________________
______________________	______________________
______________________	______________________
______________________	______________________
______________________	______________________

BECOMING YOUR HABITS

After you have read *Atomic Habits*, choose the most important habit you want to change or establish and work on it first. Work on one or two habits at a time so you do not become overwhelmed. I used to make my bed only occasionally, usually when I knew someone was coming to visit. Now, I make my bed every morning because it makes me feel better about myself. Lately, I have succeeded in getting my husband to do it too! He saw my habit and started to help each morning. He was not forced; he just started helping because I did it every day. This practice is called modeling. If you are a parent of small children, you may have noticed them imitating the things you do regularly. Children do not know the difference between good and bad habits until someone tells them. Perhaps your parents were not good role models for you. If that is the case, your coach, counselor, or therapist can help you decide what kinds of habits will work best for you.

In the space below, list some of the bad habits you want to break. Next to each one, write a new, good habit you want to start in its place.

FOCUSING ON WHAT YOU WISH TO BECOME

What is your dream? What have you always wanted to do with your life? As a child, did you want to become something when you grew up? I love horses, so at first, I wanted to be a jockey. To ride horses fast was something I always wanted to do as a child. I never really got the opportunity until I was an adult. Think about what your passions are, or what your talents are. Focus on them and take it one step at a time until you reach your goal. It is important to have goals. They give you a direction in which to go. Be willing to make sacrifices to achieve your goals. As nineteenth-century Belgian naturalist Charles Dubois said, "The important thing is this: to be able at any moment to sacrifice what we are for what we could become." In other words, you must leave behind your old self to become your new self. That may sound daunting, but over time, it can be done.

How badly do you want to change your life? You need to want it badly enough to make any change. It took losing my brother-in-law to lung cancer for my husband to finally consider stopping smoking. Ridiculous, right? I agree. I had been begging him for years. I have always loved horses, but until I was an adult, I did not have the chance to own one. As a child I was always told we could not afford one. When I became an adult, I did everything I could to find a way to own a horse. It was not easy, and the first horse I got helped me to realize I was not ready yet, and least of all, I was not ready for the one I got. Today, I have owned four horses total, one at a time. In his book *Think and Grow Rich*,

Napoleon Hill said, "The starting point of achievement is DESIRE. Keep this in mind. Weak desire brings weak results, just as a small fire makes a small amount of heat." I always had the desire to own a horse, so I suspect that is why I have always had one during my adult life, including today as I write this book.

WHEN CHANGE IS FORCED

While I was writing this book, the world experienced one of the worst pandemics ever. COVID-19 swept the world like a wildfire. It started in China and quickly spread from there. Spain and Italy were hit extremely hard. When it reached the United States, our government systematically began to shut down the schools, malls, and any non-essential businesses. Hundreds of thousands of lives were lost in our nation alone. Others lost their jobs or livelihoods. I, too, had to adjust to the "new normal." Instead of face-to-face meetings in my networking groups, we met via Zoom over the internet. People gave themselves haircuts because barbershops and salons were considered non-essential. I'm an artist, but the art galleries were closed, and the restaurants where I had my work hanging were closed. Then, as places began to open back up, businesses were requiring their employees to wear surgical or homemade fabric masks. So, what did I do? Since I had material and sewing skills, I began to make fabric masks and sell them. This was just one way I coped with the change. I also had a great fruit and vegetable garden so I sold some of my plants and seedlings.

Things during the pandemic only got worse when police brutality led to the death of African American George Floyd. Violent protests broke out across the nation. Famous people spoke out against the violence. A lot of confusion ensued. Even worse, the suicide rate went up during the pandemic, probably because people were so depressed about losing their jobs or being stuck indoors with family members who had become violent. I became a little depressed myself, so I started to turn to alcohol for comfort. That is something no one should do. So, I decided to turn back to the Lord for my help. I began to pray almost continually every day. A calmness would come over me when I was doing what the Lord wanted me to do. I felt His energy while writing this book. Gardening and exercising are other ways I balance my life. As an artist, I am sure that creating beautiful works of art is what I was designed for. I rode my horse at times as therapy. If you are feeling a little anxious, take your dog for a walk.

That is just my story. Let us now return to my friend Carissa's story. Here she shares how change was forced upon her and she had to take action to protect her daughter and herself.

> It was when I was looking for a way to start covering college costs for my infant daughter that I discovered a beautiful baby contest. I did my homework and discovered that pageants were for all ages. I didn't feel comfortable about putting her out there, but participating would give me something I could do for myself. I had really missed performing, and this would be a way to do that, and maybe help someone else because of the vol-

unteer work that was part of the contests. My ex, however, flipped out at the thought of me doing it. He said if he could, he would shut down every beauty contest. He refused to listen to anything I said. I was awarded my first at-large regional title in 1997. My daughter was three. She came with me in a stroller as I led the first heart walk in Federal Way and the City of Hope cancer awareness walk in Auburn. Because of financial abuse, I did not have the money to attend nationals. I did not have enough from my disability income to do it on my own because I was covering household bills. I refused to give up, though, and the following spring, I applied for a different competition that had a better reputation, with a larger percentage of my score based on the interview portion, which I knew was my forte. I was excited and began looking for sponsors in our little town. I got a few, but not enough to cover everything. My ex had begun taking my daughter with him to a Hindu Christian church. I was forbidden to attend. One day, his work pager went off. He was at the other end of the house, so I picked it up and read: *Romeo, where are you?!*

He was cheating on me. It cut worse than any knife. He also began taking off for days at a time, and on three separate occasions, he took our daughter with him and was gone for more than three days each time. He had a cell phone but refused to answer when I called…multiple times. By the third disappearance, I was going out of my mind with worry. He refused to tell me where he was going, or where he was taking our daughter. I called the crisis clinic…and the police. A friend of mine was an officer. He told me I was in a domestic violence situation and that my ex was preparing to take our daughter and go for good. I hadn't called the police before, even after the physical or sexual violence I experienced, because I didn't realize how serious things were. My friend said I either had to get my daughter and get out, or my soon-to-be-ex would take her and disappear. My ex had been part of special forces in the military. He had been trained on how to hide, as well as how to kill and leave no marks of murder. (He used to demonstrate on my body where he would do it.) I knew the seriousness of the situation. He brought my daughter back late that night and I put her to bed immediately. Afterward, I sat quietly in the darkness of her room for about half an hour. I was terrified that if I left the room, he would kill me and hide my body where no one would find it. My daughter would never know what had happened. He would tell her I had abandoned her. That hurt the most because I had nearly given my life to have her. When I finally prayed and left the room that night, I found he had turned off every light in the house. I should not have been surprised…. He always said the darkness was his friend and "activated his Spidey-sense." The air was so heavy I could barely breathe. Fear and something else I could not name permeated everything. Later, I recognized that unknown quantity was EVIL. I walked to the kitchen and got my nighttime meds. He was out in the living room, pacing like a caged animal does.

“We need to chat.”

His voice floated across the darkness.

“I will be right there.”

I swallowed my meds and headed out to the living room. I do not remember if I was sitting or standing as he gave me the ultimatum. He wanted me out, and I was to leave her behind. If I did as he said, he would allow me to do daycare for her. If I crossed his wishes in any way, that would not be allowed. He wanted me out by June 1, and he did not care if I was homeless. I tried to talk him out of it. Tried to get him to try to make things work. He was adamant. This was how it would be. He was gone in a couple of hours…off to his girlfriend’s. I took the calendar and circled a day in red. No notation. I would know what it was. My Freedom Day. I stopped making any attempt at cleaning the house and began putting away things I wanted to keep so I could put them in storage. By not cleaning, I hoped that anything missing would be less obvious. I gathered some of my paperwork but knew I could not take much. I tried for days to covertly find safe shelter for our two greyhounds. There was no one able to foster them. I kept trying until the last minute. When the day arrived, he showed up unexpectedly to “take us to preschool co-op.”

My fear level was off the charts. I was terrified he knew something was up, but I also knew that any deviation from our normal schedule would result in violence or worse. I was in the living room when I was raped for the last time. Along with my tears came the knowledge that this was the last time he could do this. When it was over, he walked out to the car to wait for us. I grabbed my daughter in her car seat and headed out. Once we got to class, he disappeared for a while.... I was able to tell the preschool teacher we were leaving. She added making gak [a type of slime or Play-Doh] to the day's schedule...something we could take with us to help deal with stress. Nothing was said but our short, whispered conversation, but I knew she was doing what she could to help.

After class was out, he was back. I could not shake him! I did my best performance for an Oscar.... He took us to lunch at Pizza Hut. It was like eating cardboard that stuck in my stomach, unmoving. Finally, he dropped us at the house and left. Would he be back? I had no way of knowing if he was around the block or actually headed to work.... I waited a bit, then took my daughter to a neighbor's house to watch. I made her promise she wouldn't give my daughter to him if anything happened...and returned to the house to pack up my stereo and get stuff into storage. Later, I would lose everything in the storage because he refused to let me know they had contacted him about a late fee. Everything was auc-

> tioned off out of state, including my bike (which was a special frame geometry, specifically to help with my disabilities), all my professional clothing, my jewelry and pictures and portfolio from my modeling days. It also included my daughter's Diamondback bike. There is a special place in hell for storage managers who profit off the meager possessions of women fleeing violence. Right next to abusers. Mine not only abused us but cost one of my greyhounds his life. I had contacted another friend who was the director of a domestic violence shelter in Tacoma, and we had space there.... Once I had things in storage, I put my daughter in the front of her double stroller and a small suitcase and diaper bag in the back. I grabbed my purse and headed out. As I walked out the door that last time, I wondered how to explain all this to my three-year-old (who was light years ahead verbally) and finally told her: "We are going on an adventure. I don't know where we will go, but I will make sure you are safe." She still remembers this.

SUMMARY

In this chapter, we discussed coping with change. When making any lasting changes, you will want to start with the small stuff. Then, we worked on forming good and healthy habits. These are things that will help you move on to be a better you. You will become your habits by choice because you will see positive changes in your life. Finally, we discussed focusing on what you wish to become. I said it before and I will say it again: You have control over your own destiny. It all starts with what you want out of life. It depends on how badly you want it.

In the next chapter, we will explore transformation. We will discuss where you will have to make changes, what those changes may look like, and how to get started. We will talk about your options, choosing the right path for you, and how to make plans. We will also talk about the benefits of journaling. You have come a long way just to get here. Do not give up now; good things are just around the corner.

1. How did you feel when reading this chapter?

2. What new insights did you discover about yourself while working through this chapter?

3. What new discoveries about others and the world around you did you find?

4. What do you plan on doing next or doing differently in the future?

Chapter 11

Embracing Transformation

"Transformation is not a future event. It is a present activity."

—Jillian Michaels

In the last chapter, we discussed coping with change. When making any lasting changes, you want to start with the small stuff. We worked on forming good and healthy habits that will help you move on to become a better you. You will become your habits by choice because you will see positive changes in your life. Finally, we discussed focusing on what you wish to become. As I've said before, you have control over your own destiny. It all starts with what you want out of life. It depends on how badly you want it.

In this chapter, we will explore transformation; to transform, you must make changes, so we will discuss what those changes may look like and how to get started. We will talk about your options, choosing the right path for you, and how to make plans. We will also talk about journaling and its usefulness. You have come a long way just to get here. Please do not give up now; good things are just around the corner.

EXPLORING OPTIONS

Even as I write this book, my life is going through transformations. I currently have a retail job, but by the time I finish this book, I hope to be on my way to a new career. I am an artist and photographer, so I plan to embark on a new career in real estate photography. It is competitive, so it will not be easy. I may have to work for free to build a portfolio of work. Being a creative person, I think this path will be more fulfilling than my retail job. My point is many options are available to you. If one option does not work for you, try another. Then keep on trying until you find something that works for you. As I finish up this book, I have been exploring the craft market experience. It is much like retail; it has its ups and downs. It has been another way of stepping outside my comfort zone.

So, now that you know you have options, explore them thoroughly. Find someone who is in the know, someone who has been there and done that, and ask them for some tips. That is exactly what I did. You can always google "What does it take to be a good at…?" and fill in whatever it is you want to do or be. You may be surprised by what you find. Your passion could become your career path.

CHOOSING A PATH

Everyone has a different path. The right path for you may not be the right path for someone else. You must decide what is right for you personally. I tried several career paths before

I settled on my passion for art and photography. Obviously, I also have a passion to tell my story and help others who have been sexually abused. Be patient; finding the right path for you may take some time. It may take longer than you think. You may try going back to school, getting a GED, or even attending college. You may be surprised by the number of scholarships available if you just learn where to look. It took me decades to gain the confidence to write this book, not to mention start a business.

I recommend you explore careers that can give you the income you desire. More importantly, explore careers in a field or subject you enjoy. If you love the work you do, chances are you will never regret going to work every day. You may have to reinvent yourself and/or reeducate yourself. For example, as I mentioned earlier, when the pandemic hit, reinventing myself became a necessity. The process of writing this book has been another form of reeducating myself. I hired a publishing coach who had written a book of his own as a part of reinventing himself.

MAKING PLANS

Let us return to my friend Carissa's story. Here she responded to my request for advice on how to get out of a domestic violence situation. Her response is appropriate for this chapter because she advocates planning ahead.

> Set aside some clothing, documents that will be helpful to you, and money if you can. Remember that no

material thing is more valuable than your life. If things escalate, be ready to get out sooner if needed. Put your emergency stash (clothes, money, and papers) in a safe place where you can access it when needed. If you work, leave it in your locker, leave it with a friend, or put it in the trunk of your car if you have your own vehicle. Remember, the most important thing is to get out safely. If you cannot get your important papers out, you can get other copies.

Getting out takes time. Once you are in a shelter, the people there can help you know the procedure and where to go for this help. Shelters also have access to clothing that has been donated for survivors. You can make it even if you must leave with just the clothes on your back. The safest place to go is a domestic violence confidential shelter. These are confidential locations with group settings. They offer a safe, temporary place to stay, and access to needed short-term help. Going to a family or friend's house is not recommended because it can endanger you, anyone you are staying with, or anyone who knows where you are. Do not underestimate the seriousness of your situation. Do the best you can to be safe.

Shelters have twenty-four-hour staff onsite for emergency assistance, plus they have bulletproof doors with security locks and cameras, opened only for residents or staff, unless there is a subpoena (which does not happen). They also have quick access to law enforcement, fire departments, and paramedics. Contact potential sources of assistance (domestic violence shelter and victim support organizations) when it is safe to do so. In the United States, there are twenty-four-hour hotlines at both local shelters and at the National Domestic Violence Hotline (1-800-799-SAFE). If you do not know of shelters in your area, you can go to your local public library and google "Domestic violence shelters in ________ (your area)." It is always best to use the internet in a place other than your home or to use your cell phone. Keystroke programs and other forms of cyber-stalking enable abusers to know where you have been and what you have accessed unless you use a VPN.

The National Domestic Violence Hotline also has an online support program with limited hours of operation that can help you to hook up with local help. Your local shelter program may be full when seeking space, but keep calling them! Three times a day is good. The advocates expect multiple calls. They do not know when space will become available. When people break rules (spending time with the abuser, or using drugs or alcohol, for example), they are kicked out, leaving an opening if you are quick. Once you are pre-screened and given verbal space, you have a limited amount of time to get to the shelter. They will help you make it happen once you get close by. All of that is explained when you are screened.

Once in a shelter, you will do an intake meeting with staff, have rules explained, and be given a place to sleep and other basic assistance. In some shelters, you have your own bedroom for your family. In others, sleeping is dormitory style, with multiple people/families in a room. Food is provided, along with a kitchen for preparing meals. Each resident is expected to perform some chores (usually these change weekly) and attend mandatory classes (including things like how to recognize red flag warning signs of abusive people, how to help your kids heal after abuse, self-care, survivor support groups, and more.) Children spend their days in daycare, and there are children's advocates who will stay with your children while you are at mandatory classes or other meetings. You will work with staff to come up with goals to accomplish during your stay (examples include getting an order of protection, filing for child support and custody or divorce, getting DSHS benefits, and more.) There is a curfew, so unless you are working, you need to be home before that time. Work is a valid excuse, but you need to let staff know you have work and what hours. No recreational drugs or alcohol are allowed in the shelter. If you go out, get high, and come back, expect consequences. A "normal" shelter stay is twenty-eight days. Exceptions may be made for a good cause, but you will have to follow proper procedure to see if you can get an extension.

JOURNALING

Journaling could be especially useful in your healing process. It also could help your counselor or therapist understand you and your thought patterns so they can better diagnose your current mental health. With journaling, if you start at the beginning and use it all the way through the process of healing, you can look back later to see the progress you have made. I did extensive journaling during my healing, and recently, when I looked back at some of it, I was shocked to see how messed up I felt about myself at the beginning. I realized that now I am no longer that person. My confidence has skyrocketed since then. People who want to lose weight often journal about what they eat, how much they eat, calorie content, etc. If they are emotional eaters because they are covering up some other issue like low self-esteem, journaling can help them understand their habits and patterns. This process can help them discover why they eat the way they do. People can also journal about their emotions to see if certain emotions are connected to certain events or to look for behavior patterns. Journaling about meeting new people can help the writer to understand how they felt about them or how they might get along with them.

SUMMARY

In this chapter, we explored transformation, where you will have to make changes, what those changes may look like, and how to get started. With this information, you are ready to get started. We also talked about your options, choosing the right path for you, and how to make plans. Finally, we talked about journaling and its usefulness. You have come a long way just to get this far. Please do not give up now. I want to encourage you to keep moving forward. I am sure good things are just around the corner for you.

In the next chapter, we will discuss the many aspects of art therapy. We will talk about choosing a medium (type of art or material to use) and assigning colors to emotions. We will also discuss the limitations involved with this kind of therapy. We will even consider music therapy. When it comes to therapy for children, art therapy is often where therapists start. Sometimes art is the only way children can express themselves when they've experienced abuse.

1. How did you feel when reading this chapter?

2. What new insights did you discover about yourself while working through this chapter?

3. What new discoveries about others and the world around you did you find?

4. What do you plan on doing next or doing differently in the future?

Chapter 12

Exploring Art Therapy

"Art can permeate the very deepest part of us, where no words exist."

— Eileen Miller

In the last chapter, we explored transformation, including where you will have to make changes, what those changes may look like, and how to get started. With this information, you are ready to get started on your transformation. We also talked about your options, choosing the right path for you, and how to make plans. Finally, we discussed the usefulness of journaling. You have come a long way now, so please do not give up. I encourage you to keep moving forward. I am sure good things are just around the corner for you.

In this chapter, we will discuss the many aspects of art therapy. We will talk about choosing an art medium and assigning colors to emotions. We will also discuss the limitations involved with this kind of therapy. Finally, we will consider music therapy. For children, art therapy is often the place to start because art may be the only way children can express themselves about the abuse.

WHAT IS ART THERAPY?

Since I am an artist, I want to delve into this subject. I have found art therapy useful in my personal healing process. Art therapy is a way to express yourself without using words. It can also help the therapist understand what you may be experiencing without you having to say a word. I am not discounting talk therapy; I am just saying that art therapy is a way to start in some cases. As an expressive medium, art can be used to help clients communicate, overcome stress, and explore different aspects of their own personalities.

What exactly is art therapy? On verywellmind.com, The American Art Therapy Association describes art therapy as an approach to mental health that uses the process of creating art to improve mental, physical, and emotional wellness. Art therapist and author Cathy Malchiodi states in *The Art Therapy Sourcebook* that art therapy is "based on the idea that the creative process of art making is healing and life enhancing, and that it is a potent form of communication. It utilizes the creative process...to promote growth, self-expression, emotional reparation, conflict resolution and transformation." Art therapy is often the best way to start communication with a young child who has been traumatized and will not speak or does not know how to write yet. Looking at someone else's art—at a museum, gallery, or studio—may provide a similar emotional release for someone who has experienced trauma. Sometimes viewing others' creative works can help us heal through the message evoked or the medium used.

For additional resources on art therapy and its benefits and uses, please consult:

https://www.verywellmind.com/what-is-art-therapy-2795755

https://www.heysigmund.com/art-therapy/

http://thewestreichfoundation.org/creative-arts-and-consciousness-arts-in-healing/

https://www.canyonranch.com/blog/mind-and-spirit/art-therapy-healing-through-self-expression/

https://www.utne.com/arts/art-therapy-ze0z1311zcalt

CHOOSING A MEDIUM

Many of the techniques used in art therapy can include drawing, painting, coloring, sculpting, or collage. The hard part may be deciding which one to use. Of course, you do not have to have any artistic talent to try art therapy. Many companies that produce coloring books are today catering to adults who like to color but are not very artistic themselves. Just working with abstract colors may help you get your emotions across. What is important is that you choose a medium you are comfortable with. When I was exploring art therapy, I liked to use colored pencils and colored marker pens. It made it easy to switch colors, and drawing this way was fast because I never knew how long an inspiration would last. I would recommend getting an inexpensive art kit and trying everything in it before you decide which to use. However, you can also combine several types of media. There is drawing, painting, sculpture, carving, and all variations of each to choose from.

ASSIGN COLORS TO YOUR EMOTIONS

It will help your therapist if you assign colors to each of your emotions. For instance, red for anger, blue for sadness, yellow for fright, green for envy, purple for happiness, or whatever colors you like for each emotion. If you are colorblind or cannot distinguish between two colors, try using shapes to identify your emotions. My art contained a lot of red and black, indicating a lot of anger and depression. Those were the colors I used the most because they were the emotions I was working through the most.

To help your therapist or counselor, draw a few pictures of how you feel using the colors you have chosen. In the blank pages provided, explore your emotions with the colors and imagery of your choice.

LIMITATIONS

While research suggests that art therapy may be beneficial, some of the findings on its effectiveness are mixed. Studies are often small and inconclusive, so further research is needed to explore how and when art therapy may be most beneficial. Therefore, there may be certain limitations on how effective this therapy will be for you. In my opinion, you get what you put into it. The more of yourself that you put into your art, the better the results.

MUSIC THERAPY

What is music therapy? Music therapy is the clinical and evidence-based use of music interventions to accomplish individualized goals within a therapeutic relationship by a credentialed professional who has completed an approved music therapy program. The concept of music therapy is believed to have been around since the time of Plato and Aristotle. A paper published in 1789 titled "Music Physically Considered" contains the earliest known mentions of using music as a healing tool.

Music therapy interventions can be designed to:

- Promote wellness
- Manage stress
- Alleviate pain
- Express feelings
- Enhance memory

- Improve communication
- Promote physical rehabilitation

"With individuals who have experienced trauma," says Jim Borling, director of Radford University's Music Therapy program, "music becomes an outlet for expressing emotion. Music therapy has a way of letting people know that it is ok to feel what you are feeling. It is ok to acknowledge what has happened."[15]

Every person's physical and emotional trauma experiences are unique, so each therapeutic treatment will be as well. The role of the music therapist is to encourage and allow the patient to express themselves in a safe environment. In her published article "Music Therapy with Sexually Abused Children," Jacqueline Robarts of Nordoff-Robbins Music Therapy Centre (UK) wrote about the case of Sally, who was sexually abused as a child. Robarts recounted her music therapy sessions with Sally, where she described "recreative processes that were set in motion to help repair the damage done to the child during the formative stages of her development; how the medium of music played a vital role in helping her recover—or rather build—a bodily, emotional and mental sense of self."[16]

SUMMARY

In this chapter, we discussed the many aspects of art therapy. We explored choosing a medium and assigning colors to emotions. We also talked about the limitations involved with this kind of therapy. We even considered music therapy and how it can be helpful. Finally, we discussed how art therapy is often the best way to help children begin to express themselves regarding abuse. While more research is needed on the benefits of art and music therapy, I honestly believe in their usefulness.

In the next chapter, we will talk about overcoming limiting beliefs. These include limiting thoughts about yourself and the world and how they have influenced aspects of your life. We will explore creating positive mantras and how powerful they can be. We will talk about the importance of changing your thought patterns to help you build self-confidence. We will also explore stepping out of your comfort zone. Finally, we will talk about finding your inner strengths and personal attributes.

1. How did you feel when reading this chapter?

2. What new insights did you discover about yourself while working through this chapter?

3. What new discoveries about others and the world around you did you find?

4. What do you plan on doing next or doing differently in the future?

Chapter 13

Overcoming Limiting Beliefs

"You begin to fly when you let go of self-limiting beliefs and allow your mind and aspirations to rise to greater heights."

— Brian Tracy

In the last chapter, we discussed the many aspects of art therapy. We explored how to choose a medium and assign colors to emotions. We also talked about the limitations involved with this kind of therapy. We even considered music therapy and how it can be helpful. When it comes to therapy for children, art therapy is often where they start. With children, sometimes this is the only way they can express themselves about the abuse. More research is needed on this form of therapy, but I genuinely believe in its usefulness.

In this chapter, we will talk about overcoming limiting beliefs. These include limiting thoughts about yourself and the world and how they have influenced aspects of your life.

We will explore creating positive mantras and how powerful they can be. Next, we will talk about the importance of changing your thought patterns to help you build self-confidence. We will also explore stepping out of your comfort zone. Finally, we will talk about finding your inner strengths and personal attributes.

BELIEFS ABOUT YOURSELF AND THE WORLD

When we are growing up, many of us take on the limiting beliefs of our parents and caretakers. Too often, we are told by those who have the most influence over us that we are just not good enough or we will never amount to anything. First, *no* adult has *any* right to say that to *any* child. Every child born has the potential to become whatever they want in life. Sometimes the abusers are siblings. In any case, the victims often feel like they have no value or influence over their own lives. Even if no one said those things to you, you may have felt that way because of your physically or sexually abusive experiences.

Now is the time for all of that to change. It's time to start thinking positively about yourself. You can do anything you want in life if you want it badly enough. Negative thoughts bring negative results; positive thoughts bring positive results. I realize if you are still in the middle of your healing process, thinking positive thoughts may be a little difficult. It was for me. But in time, it will get easier.

CREATING POSITIVE MANTRAS

What is a mantra? In this context, a mantra is a positive phrase, statement, or slogan that is repeated frequently. Positive mantras are good for the healing process. Here are a few you can use for your healing process:

- I give myself permission to heal.
- I am willing to forgive myself.
- I am ready to forgive anyone I feel has hurt me.

These mantras, if repeated enough, can eventually change the way you feel about yourself. Let us try creating some positive mantras of our own. Start with the words "I am" and use the present tense. Keep the sentence brief and specific. Include an action word ending in "ing" and at least one emotion or feeling. For example:

- I am worthy of love.
- I am going to be successful.
- I am useful and productive.
- My life is prospering.
- My life has meaning.
- I am doing good works.

CHANGING YOUR THOUGHT PATTERNS

In his popular book *Think and Grow Rich,* Napoleon Hill taught that "our brains become magnetized with the dominating thoughts which we hold in our minds, and by means with which no man is familiar, these 'magnets' attract us to forces, the people, the circumstances, of the life which harmonize with the nature of our dominating thoughts." Norman Vincent Peale added in *The Power of Positive Thinking*, "The person who sends out positive thoughts activates the world around him positively and draws back to himself positive results." I believe this is true. I personally have noticed that when I am in a good mood or in a positive attitude, my day seems to go a lot smoother; things turn out better.

STEPPING OUT OF YOUR COMFORT ZONE

Stepping out of your comfort zone can be as scary as it sounds—at least it was for me. My friend Carissa is a beauty pageant champion. She managed to talk me into stepping out of my comfort zone by joining a pageant competition. But it was not just a beauty pageant. Writing an essay was also involved, as well as an interview. The competitors all had some sort of platform for social change or awareness. My platform was sexual abuse awareness and help for victims. I joined the competition so I could get more exposure for my book and, hopefully, a speaking and workshop tour or build a coaching business. I claimed the title of Mrs. Ireland to compete in the Elite Queen Classic Beauty International. I picked Ireland because I have some Irish in my ethnic background and I have always been interested in Irish history. Someday, I would like to travel to Ireland to see and photograph the castles. Meanwhile, I completed writing this book in 2021, still during the pandemic. Now, it's time to promote it, which is scary, to say the least.

Before I became willing to step out of my comfort zone, I had trouble meeting new people. One time, I joined a small business networking group. I was in that group for months before I started getting to know anyone. I eventually became more confident in my abilities to speak in front of a group. Now I plan on joining a local Toastmasters group to meet people and improve my public speaking skills.

INNER STRENGTHS AND PERSONAL ATTRIBUTES

Everyone has some sort of inner strength or a personal attribute that makes up their character—a natural talent that lies within. What is it you are passionate about? What is it you like to do the most? What can you do well that might benefit someone else? These things are your inner strengths and personal attributes.

Let's return to my friend Carissa. I've asked her here to share with us how she found her own calling and followed it.

> I knew from the time I was in the shelter that I would be helping other women one day. The things I have learned the hard way can help someone else if they get the information. It changes everything when we are no longer alone. That isolation is a huge tool abusers use against their victims. That is one reason I am excited about getting survivors together and helping them realize they have the tools to heal and reach for their own success:

their destiny. Much of what I teach I learned the hard way, going through it all alone. If it can help someone else, I am happy to help, and I found a great side effect: helping others helps me heal.

I have been giving back, volunteering in my community for more than half my life. I know how powerful helping others can be, both in supporting the community and in personal growth and skill and confidence-building. It also helps connect people in ways that can aid them in building a successful future. Women working together have the potential to be one of the most powerful forces on the planet. Yes, I am speaking from personal experience. If you asked me years ago, I never would have dreamed I would have the privilege of working with a group of amazing women activists. This activism has been separate from my work on domestic violence issues, but dovetails it. We are here on the planet to make a difference. Part of that means doing what we can to help others along their way. This becomes even more important in survivors' lives. Many use pieces of the system and domestic violence victim support organizations to help them get and stay safe. Giving back is a natural progression. Someone put a hand out to help you up…and you return the favor. If you have not done it before, know that it is a life-changing experience. Definitely a win-win.

What does my future look like? I am excited about what is coming, and I am working hard to put things in place to make them work for my daughter and me. In addition to my book, I am also writing a curriculum for my healing and success program, designed to help women move from victim to survivor to thriver. It's about healing, self-discovery, skill-building, and success. For now, I will be starting with online "virtual" classes, working with a group of women I have supported…in some cases for a number of years through online advocacy at the Power of Being Free group. I do a lot of mentoring, and this program will just officially take things to the next level. The program will be my way of giving back, and as one of my favorite inspirations says, "my way of paying rent for being on the planet."

I am also working on building my public speaking opportunities, as well as doing video blogging, internet radio and film projects; writing articles and blogs; and doing research. My hope is that things will calm down pandemic-wise and my health will stabilize so I can continue my education, first by finishing those last four courses to have my bachelor's degree complete, and second by looking at graduate school. Not sure if it will be a master's or doctorate program…maybe law school. Going to school was an outgrowth of my advocacy work. I knew I needed to be well prepared to tackle the challenges coming my way. I started college at age seventeen, but it took me about forty-four years to finally finish my degree. I was told I have a natural aptitude for law and would love to pursue it if possible.

> We will see what the future holds. My greatest passion is making a difference. I have many ways to pursue it, but the underlying purpose is the same.

In the lines below, list what you feel are your personal strengths and attributes.

SUMMARY

In this chapter, we talked about overcoming limiting beliefs. These beliefs include limiting thoughts about yourself and the world and how they have influenced aspects of your life. We explored creating positive mantras and how powerful they can be. We also talked about the importance of changing your thought patterns to help you build self-confidence. We even explored stepping out of your comfort zone and what that might feel like. Finally, we talked about finding your inner strength and personal attributes.

In the next chapter, we will explore risk management. First, we will identify unhealthy risks and how to avoid them. Also, we will talk about implementing healthy risks. To move forward and grow as a human, you may need to take some risks. Next, we will talk about learning to trust again. Learning to trust again is a terribly slow but extremely important process. Finally, we will explore the difference between sexual harassment and sexual abuse.

1. How did you feel when reading this chapter?

2. What new insights did you discover about yourself while working through this chapter?

3. What new discoveries about others and the world around you did you find?

4. What do you plan on doing next or doing differently in the future?

Chapter 14

Risk Management

"If you are not willing to risk the unusual, you will have to settle for the ordinary."

—Jim Rohn

In the last chapter, we talked about overcoming limiting beliefs. These beliefs include limiting thoughts about yourself and the world and how they have influenced aspects of your life. We explored creating positive mantras and how powerful they can be. We also talked about the importance of changing your thought patterns to help you build self-confidence. We explored stepping out of your comfort zone and what that might feel like. Finally, we talked about finding your inner strength and personal attributes.

In this chapter, we will explore risk management. First, we will identify unhealthy risks and how to avoid them. Also, we will talk about implementing healthy risks. To move forward and grow as a human, you may need to take some risks.

Next, we will talk about learning to trust again. Finally, we will explore the difference between sexual harassment and sexual abuse. I realize these are difficult subjects to deal with, but they are all important for creating a happy, healthy, and whole you.

UNHEALTHY RISKS

There are many risks to take out there in the world, so you need to know which ones to avoid. Some risks are considered unhealthy, like walking in the big city late at night alone; not many people would voluntarily do that if given a choice. Smoking cigarettes is also a big risk, although you may not experience the consequences for many years. Unhealthy risks to avoid as a survivor of sexual abuse would include drinking alcohol when you are already depressed. Instead, call a trusted friend or counselor to talk about how you are feeling. Another unhealthy risk would be going to bars in neighborhoods that you would not bring kids to. Duh! Kind of obvious. These are the places where the people you will want to avoid will often go—people who may tempt you into drinking alcohol or taking illicit drugs. Taking such risks will hinder your healing process.

IMPLEMENTING HEALTHY RISKS

Depending on how far you are in the healing process, it may be time to start implementing healthy risks, like deciding on a counselor to open up to, looking for new friends, or even moving to a new neighborhood or starting a new job.

For me, a healthy risk was participating in the virtual beauty pageant. I knew it was one way I could practice and improve my speaking skills. It was also an opportunity to boost my confidence. A healthy risk could include joining a church, which I mentioned in a previous chapter. This may also be a good time to join a health club. Your primary healthy risk there is meeting new people, but at the same time, you are improving your health.

LEARNING TO TRUST AGAIN

It took me an awfully long time to trust anyone again—anyone other than my husband, my children, and of course, my parents. In 2001, I took a volunteer internship at a local radio station. I worked in the promotions department where I had the opportunity to create radio commercials. One day when I was working in the recording booth on a commercial, the sports personality, thinking he was being cute, snapped my bra strap. I considered that a form of sexual assault, so I almost punched him. I did yell at him and tell him he better not try it again! I made an official report, but I felt like nothing was done to punish him. It caused me digestive issues due to all the anxiety I was having. I eventually had to leave that position because I was fairly sure it wouldn't lead to a paid position. After leaving that position, I went to a women's self-defense class offered by a blackbelt in Taekwondo. That one class was not enough for me to remember how to protect myself, so I joined a Taekwondo school. Thirteen years later, and with a third degree blackbelt, I am now confident in my ability to protect myself. Eventually, after two ACL replacements in my knees, the doctors told me to stop Taekwondo. That was a sad day, but I had to listen to them. Regardless, I can protect myself if needed.

I highly recommend you take a self-defense class of some sort to learn how to protect yourself. Knowing how to protect yourself will make you feel more empowered and confident. I chose Taekwondo out of convenience; the class just happened to be nearby and was recommended by a counselor. I also chose it because it was a great way to exercise. Please consult your doctor before starting any kind of rigorous activities.

I still have trust issues, but I am getting better at giving people the benefit of the doubt and try to get to know them better before I judge their characters. This may be a good time to review your list of trusted and supportive people. Is there anyone you can add to the list? Is there anyone you should take off the list after further examination?

THE DIFFERENCE BETWEEN SEXUAL ABUSE AND SEXUAL HARRASSMENT

According to sexualviolence.ucla.edu, "Sexual Violence means physical sexual acts without the consent of the other person or when the other person is unable to give consent. Sexual violence includes sexual assault, rape, domestic violence, dating violence and stalking." Sexual violence can also be called sexual abuse. The difference between sexual abuse or violence and sexual harassment can be a fine line. I always thought sexual harassment was something that happened at work or school, but now I realize it is more complicated. According to sexualviolence.ucla.edu:

> Sexual Harassment includes behavior such as unwelcome sexual advances, requests for sexual favors, and other conduct of a sexual nature. It is conduct that affects a person's employment or education or interferes with a person's work or educational performance or creates an environment that a reasonable person would find intimidating, hostile or offensive.

Sexual abuse is usually connected to something that happens to children, which is the primary focus of this book—the healing of adults and teens who have been sexually abused as children. Forms of sexual abuse include exposing oneself to a child, sexual contact with a minor including fondling and intercourse, obscene messages, pornography, and sex trafficking. I would like to include anything that makes you uncomfortable or causes your gut instinct to tell you to *run*. You can find more information at:

https://www.sexualviolence.ucla.edu/FAQs/Understanding-Sexual-Violence-and-Sexual-Assault

SUMMARY

In this chapter, we explored risk management. First, we identified unhealthy risks and how to avoid them. Then we talked about implementing healthy risks. To move forward and grow as a human, you may need to take some risks. Next, we talked about learning to trust again. Finally, we explored the difference between sexual harassment and sexual abuse. I realize these are difficult topics; if you need to, take some time to think about what you read, or reread the chapter before moving on to the next one.

In the next chapter, we will talk about how to reward yourself for a job well done, even if it is a small win. We will discuss how to take what you have learned and use it to become a leader. Also, we will revisit Carissa's story of how she is using her experiences to help others and become a leader in the domestic violence awareness movement. Finally, we will talk about how to find your happiness. What makes someone happy is different for each person.

1. How did you feel when reading this chapter?

2. What new insights did you discover about yourself while working through this chapter?

3. What new discoveries about others and the world around you did you find?

4. What do you plan on doing next or doing differently in the future?

Chapter 15

Achieving Happiness

"The secret of being happy is accepting where you are in life and making the most out of every day."

— Anonymous

In the last chapter, we explored risk management. We talked about the difference between healthy and unhealthy risks. We identified unhealthy risks and how to avoid them. Also, we talked about implementing healthy risks. To move forward and grow as a human, you may need to take some risks. Then, we talked about learning to trust again. Lastly, we explored the difference between sexual harassment and sexual abuse. I realize these are difficult subjects to deal with. Take your time to work through the healing process.

In this chapter, we will talk about how to reward yourself for a job well done, even if it is a small win. We will discuss how to take what you have learned and use it to become a leader. Also, we will revisit Carissa's story of how she is using her experiences to help others and become a leader in the domestic violence awareness movement. Finally, we will talk about how to find your happiness. What makes someone happy is different for each person.

REWARDING YOURSELF

When you achieve a specific goal, you should reward yourself. Rewarding yourself can be your motivation to continue in any endeavor. If you have lost weight, the reward should be a new wardrobe. Likewise, the reward for a hard day's work could be a paycheck or recognition. Perhaps your goal was lowering your blood pressure. Reward yourself with a scenic walk or hike, maybe a bike ride. As Jonas Salk, developer of the polio vaccine, once said, "The reward for work well done is the opportunity to do more."

Another way to reward yourself is to take a vacation. It does not have to be an expensive one. There are budget-friendly options from a weekend camping close to home to visiting a relative in the next state. Whatever you decide, plan it, prepare for it, and enjoy yourself. Bring a trusted friend along to share and record it with you.

BECOMING A LEADER

"A genuine leader is not a searcher of consensus, but a molder of consensus."

— Martin Luther King, Jr.

Let us return to my friend Carissa's story. Here I asked her to talk more about her calling and passion.

> My formal platform is Advocacy Without Borders. I am an advocate for vulnerable people, an expert on domestic violence issues, and have pioneered work in domestic violence cyberadvocacy since 2006. I am a survivor of child abuse, domestic violence and disabilities, and a voice for those who have no voice, including the impoverished, disabled, and seniors, as well as domestic violence, sexual assault, and child abuse victims.
>
> I was disabled because of a car crash in 1983, playing "sandwich" between a truck and a full-sized car. The Mustang II Mach I was driving was totaled, and I went from full-time employment during the day, plus being a full-time music artist at night, to not being able to do anything. It was a challenging journey, and I had to find a reason to keep going and a way to put the broken pieces back together in a way that fit. The domestic violence relationship I survived took place after being disabled. Once I got out and started over, I began reaching out to give others the help I didn't have in the process. Being a survivor, as well as a professional, gives me a unique perspective and allows me to use my own experiences, as well as significant knowledge gained in the field, to make a positive difference.
>
> In addition to direct victim support services and referrals, I work legislatively at the (Washington State)

level and with the United States Congress, including participating in press conferences and testifying before judicial and congressional hearings. I have been invited to testify before the United States Congress, and my story has been told on the floor of the United States Senate during debate on the Violence Against Women Act (VAWA) reauthorization in 2012 and 2013. I am currently waiting until after the fall 2020 election to see if we will be actively working on getting the Violence Against Women Act updated and authorized. We have been without a new bill or a reauthorization of VAWA now for more than three years, despite a good bill that was passed by the House of Representatives months ago.

I speak publicly in addition to my legislative work, and I help facilitate needed changes in laws, focusing on victim safety and support areas, social justice, and civil and human rights. I write magazine articles, as well as maintain an online presence (which will be expanded soon) in addition to writing books. I am a vlogger and an interviewee for radio online, as well as doing occasional live streaming. This is another area I will be expanding in the near future. I collaborate with global mainstream media to educate the public and work for change to better protect children, victims, and survivors of abuse, poverty, and injustice. To that end, I work with radio and television broadcasting as a spokeswoman in addition to creating independent films. My media resume includes: Forbes.com and women's e-news (interna-

> tional); *USA Today*; Maria Shriver's shriverreport.org; *Seattle Times*; KING, KIRO, KOMO, and Q13 television news; womenforjustice.us; firesteel.org; café-mom; and more. One of my goals is to take my message to the highest levels, working internationally on the issues, and speaking at the United Nations.

Now let's return to Angie. Since she has been bold enough to talk about her experience, people have come to her to talk about their own stories and get her advice. She loves to help people, which she says is "my passion." Helping others is what motivates her to keep going on with her own life.

HAPPINESS IS A CHOICE

I have heard many times from other people that happiness is a choice. You must choose to be happy with yourself and your situation. I learned that I can be happy with less money because health insurance goes up according to your income. Both of my brothers currently make twice as much money as my husband and I do. When I heard how much they had to pay for their health insurance costs, I was suddenly happy with our lower income. We live in a much smaller home than either my brothers, so we pay less in taxes, and probably a smaller mortgage payment too.

Some people out there think having a lot of stuff will bring you happiness. Some people believe if you have a lot of money, you will be happy too. Not true. The more stuff you have, the more you must worry about protecting it. Same with money. The more you have, the more you must worry about saving/protecting it. You worry about people stealing your possessions. If you are not careful, you can lose your money through scams. That is just too much stuff to worry about. The important things in life are not things—they are your family, friends, and your experiences.

TAKING CARE OF YOUR BODY

If I sound like I am repeating myself, it is because I am. We have talked about this before. One particularly important aspect of healing that you don't want to forget is taking care of your body. You must offer your body good nutrition and plenty of exercise. I am no expert by any means, so I recommend you consult a physician, dietitian, or naturopathic doctor before trying anything new. The first thing I did was to eliminate sugary drinks. I switched to drinking only water and some milk. Next, I cut way down on sweets. To prevent temptation, I do not keep a lot of cookies in my house. If your body is not well fueled, your mind will not work well.

Since your brain works 24/7, including when you sleep, you should fuel it with the best quality foods. The best quality foods you can eat will help improve your mental and emotional health. In her post on the Harvard Health Blog, Eva Selhub writes:

> Serotonin is a neurotransmitter that helps regulate sleep and appetite, mediate moods, and inhibit pain. Since about 95% of your serotonin is produced in your

gastrointestinal tract, and your gastrointestinal tract is lined with a hundred million nerve cells, or neurons, it makes sense that the inner workings of your digestive system do not just help you digest food, but also guide your emotions.

You can find more information about the effect nutrition has on your brain at:

https://www.health.harvard.edu/blog/nutritional-psychiatry-your-brain-on-food-201511168626

Before starting any sort of diet or exercise program, you should consult a doctor. "The 2015-2020 Dietary Guidelines for Americans, published by the U.S. Department of Health and Human Services and the Department of Agriculture, say a healthy, balanced diet should include:

- Fruits and vegetables
- Whole grains
- Low-fat dairy
- Lean protein
- Limited amounts of sodium, saturated fat, and added sugar[17]

I know I usually feel better when I am getting enough exercise and sleep. I genuinely believe they go hand-in-hand. You really cannot get good sleep without having good exercise as well. Make sure you are getting adequate amounts of each for your health and wellbeing. These things are important to your mental and emotional health. Exercise can improve your blood flow, which is how oxygen and nutrients are moved through your body.

Let us revisit Angie's story. One way she overcame what happened to her was to get into bodybuilding. I think this is a fantastic way to recover and move forward with life. Not only did she get into bodybuilding, but she is also doing personal training, which is a way she can help others. She feels both are constructive ways to get out the pain and anger.

SUMMARY

In this chapter, we talked about how to reward yourself for a job well done, even if it is a small win. We discussed how to take what you have learned and use it to become a leader. Also, we revisited Carissa's story of how she is using her experiences to help others and to become a leader in the domestic violence awareness movement. Finally, we talked about how to find your happiness. We discovered that what makes people happy is different for each person.

We're almost done now. Just one section left to go.

1. How did you feel when reading this chapter?

2. What new insights did you discover about yourself while working through this chapter?

3. What new discoveries about others and the world around you did you find?

4. What do you plan on doing next or doing differently in the future?

A Final Note

Resting in Your Hope

"Once you have made the decision to overcome your fears, conquer all of your self-doubt and win the battle of your mind, you will accomplish everything you have ever envisioned."

— Patrick Snow

Now that you have read my book, my story, I hope you are inspired to do something to find your own hope. That has been my main goal for this book. I want to encourage others to heal themselves in whatever ways work best for them. I hope you found something useful in this book for your own journey to healing. I tried to lay it out like a set of guidelines or steps that you can take at your own pace. However, there is nothing wrong with jumping back and forth in the chapters if you feel more comfortable working that way. Besides, that is kind of how I wrote the book in the first place. You may want to go back and reread or work through some of the chapters. In fact, I encourage you to do so.

I challenge you to take action for your own healing. Yes, you can be proactive in your own healing process just as I was. Take what you have learned in this book and apply it to your life.

Here is your healing plan in fifteen steps. Each step reflects a chapter we have explored:

1. Understand What Happened to You
2. Locate Helpful Resources
3. Decide on Counseling or Therapy
4. Know It Is Not Your Fault
5. Embrace Your Inner Child
6. Be Comfortable With Yourself
7. Release Your Emotions
8. Forgive Your Transgressors
9. Move On With Your Life
10. Cope With Change
11. Embrace Transformation
12. Explore Art Therapy
13. Overcome Limiting Beliefs
14. Manage Risks
15. Achieve Happiness

In this book, you learned about what really happened to you and that it was not your fault. I showed you how to find helpful resources to guide you, as well as how to decide between counseling or therapy or both. You learned to embrace your inner child and get comfortable with yourself. We discussed releasing emotions and letting go of shame. These things are important to your health and wellbeing. I hope you get the chance to forgive those who have hurt you when you are ready. You will be amazed by how good it makes you feel. Remember, forgiving is for you, not them. Besides, you are ready to move on with life, especially if you apply the strategies I outlined in this book. For instance, stop judging all people in the same way. I want you to remember there are good people out there. You also learned about coping with change, embracing transformation, exploring art and music therapy, overcoming your limiting beliefs, and taking care of your body—all good chapters for taking care of yourself while you go through this process. In the last four chapters, I explained how you can implement risk management in a healthy way, achieve happiness, reward yourself responsibly, and become a leader. If I can do it, you can do it too!

If you apply most or all the suggestions in this book, you will succeed in healing. It does not matter how long it takes. The process will be different for each person who reads this book. Everyone heals in their own time and in their own way. I have just provided some of the tools so you can heal. I hope you have considered this to be a workbook of sorts that you wrote in and worked through at your own pace. If not, you can go back now and do the exercises or review topics you want to refresh yourself on or need to work on more.

I am so proud of you for taking this journey with me. I know it wasn't easy. I also know you have the power within you to continue to heal and thrive. You are a survivor. You are a leader. Go out there and change your life and then change your world. I am cheering you on!

Your friend,

Anne Peters

Resources

BOOKS

Bass, Ellen and Laura Davis. *The Courage to Heal: A Guide for Women Survivors of Child Sexual Abuse.*

Blume, E. Sue. *Secret Survivors: Uncovering Incest and Its Aftereffects in Women.*

Bradshaw, John. *Healing the Shame That Binds You.*

Bradshaw, John. *Homecoming: Reclaiming and Healing Your Inner Child.*

Clear, James. *Atomic Habits: An Easy and Proven Way to Build Good Habits and Break Bad Ones.*

Daugherty, Lynn. *Why Me? Help for Victims of Child Sexual Abuse*

Davis, Laura. *The Courage to Heal Workbook: A Guide for Women and Men Survivors of Child Sexual Abuse.*

Hill, Napoleon. *Think and Grow Rich.*

Malchiodi, Cathy. *The Art Therapy Sourcebook.*

Peale, Norman Vincent. *The Power of Positive Thinking.*

Sanders, Jayneen. *Some Secrets Should Never Be Kept.*

WEBSITES

Art Therapy
https://www.verywellmind.com/what-is-art-therapy-2795755

https://www.heysigmund.com/art-therapy/

http://thewestreichfoundation.org/creative-arts-and-consciousness-arts-in-healing/

https://www.canyonranch.com/blog/mind-and-spirit/art-therapy-healing-through-self-expression/

https://www.utne.com/arts/art-therapy-ze0z1311zcalt

Confronting Your Abuser
https://psychcentral.com/lib/7-ways-family-members-re-victimize-sexual-abuse-survivors#1.

Grief
https://grief.com/sexual-harassment-assault-grief/

Grooming

https://www.oprah.com/oprahshow/child-sexual-abuse-6-stages-of-grooming/

Meditation
https://suzanneheyn.com/meditation-technique-emotional-healing/

https://chopra.com/articles/healing-the-source-of-emotional-pain

https://www.pushingbeauty.com/articles/meditation-healing-emotions

Music Therapy

Robarts, Jacqueline. "Music Therapy with Sexually Abused Children." https://journals.sagepub.com/doi/pdf/10.1177/1359104506061418.

Nutrition

https://www.health.harvard.edu/blog/nutritional-psychiatry-your-brain-on-food-201511168626

Understanding Abuse

https://www.sexualviolence.ucla.edu

https://www.sexualviolence.ucla.edu/FAQs/Understanding-Sexual-Violence-and-Sexual-Assault

Endnotes

1. https://victimsofcrime.org/media/reporting-on-child-sexual-abuse/child-sexual-abuse-statistics. Accessed August 17, 2021.

2. https://chopra.com/articles/find-your-true-self-through-meditation. Accessed September 20, 2021.

3. https://www.irishexaminer.com/world/oprah-i-was-raped-when-i-was-only-9-215310.html https://www.thenationalcouncil.org/ceos-corner-office/2018/03/oprah-winfrey-healing-inside/ https://www.learning-liftoff.com/overcoming-obstacles-what-oprah-winfrey-learned-from-her-abusive-childhood/. Accessed August 26, 2021.

4. https://madamenoire.com/456634/celebs-who-overcame-sexual-abuse/4/. Accessed September 20, 2021.

5. https://madamenoire.com/456634/celebs-who-overcame-sexual-abuse/10/. Accessed August 26, 2021.

6. https://www.youtube.com/watch?v=WF4jc3Odgpg. Accessed August 26, 2021.

7. https://www.ranker.com/list/celebrities-who-were-sexually-abused/celebrity-lists. Accessed August 26, 2021.

8. https://www.insider.com/bella-thorne-childhood-sexual-abuse-poetry-book-2019-7. Accessed August 26, 2021.

9. https://www.youtube.com/watch?v=FqU4T2h-VKs. Accessed August 26, 2021.

10. https://en.wikipedia.org/wiki/Stockholm_syndrome. Accessed August 18, 2021.

11. https://www.youtube.com/watch?v=95iVuq80L68. Accessed August 26, 2021.

12. https://www.youtube.com/watch?v=dv5hTeWTLUo and https://stylecaster.com/celebrities-sexual-assault-survivor/slide1. Accessed August 26, 2021.

13. https://nickwignall.com/negative-self-talk/. Accessed August 26, 2021.

14. https://psychcentral.com/lib/7-ways-family-members-re-victimize-sexual-abuse-survivors#1. Accessed August 26, 2021.

15. https://marisapeer.com/oprah-winfrey-on-turning-wounds-into-wisdom/. Accessed September 17, 2021.

16. https://majoringinmusic.com/music-therapy-addresses-trauma. Accessed August 19, 2021.

17. https://journals.sagepub.com/doi/pdf/10.1177/1359104506061418. Accessed August 19, 2021.

18. https://familydoctor.org/nutrition-mental-health/. Accessed August 20, 2021.

About the Author

Anne Peters is an author, speaker, and healing coach. She has devoted thirty-five years to her own healing process—starting and stopping several times along the way until she found what worked for her. Next, she spent a year or so writing this book while working with her mentor.

Using her own and other people's experiences to write this book, Anne's purpose is to help others to heal from their own abuse. She is passionate about the subject and wants to help as many people as possible.

Anne has other passions too. She is an accomplished artist, illustrator, and photographer in her own right. She is featured in two local galleries and has a website with prints for sale at: petersartdesign.com.

A wife, mother, and grandmother of four, Anne loves vegetable and flower gardening, hiking, and horseback riding. She lives on five acres in rural Kitsap County in the state of Washington with her husband Timothy.

About Anne Peters Coaching

Anne Peters is a successful coach and speaker, who shares her own and other people's powerful stories to inspire and encourage survivors of abuse to overcome and succeed in life. Anne offers private one-on-one sessions over the phone or through video chat.

Having been through sexual traumas of her own, Anne understands how you are feeling. She will acknowledge and validate your feelings and help you process all that has happened to you, then encourage you to move forward. Anne is available for you to connect with and share your experience.

As you are being mentored by Anne, she will compassionately listen to your story and help you understand that what happened to you was not your fault. She will carefully guide you to the resources you need to heal.

If you are interested in being mentored by Anne, she offers a thirty-minute complimentary, no-obligation consultation to see if you would like to work with her. It doesn't matter how recent or long ago the sexual trauma was, Anne can help. Please contact her at:

FindingYourHope.com
Anne@FindingYourHope.com
(253) 225-3380

Book Anne Peters to Speak at Your Next Event

When it comes to choosing a professional speaker, you won't find anyone like Anne Peters. She is passionate and compassionate. She is known for speaking from her heart and soul, leaving her audiences inspired, empowered, and motivated to follow a new path toward their own healing process. She fills them with hope, love, and understanding as she motivates them to move forward.

Anne opens up a dialogue for healing in a way that no one else can. She shares stories of courage and triumph from her own and others' personal experiences. Her goal is to inspire, grow, and help others to see the good in themselves. Anne will deliver a message of hope and understanding, as well as transformation to motivate and empower even the most timid individual to help themselves.

Whether your group is 10 or 10,000, in the United States or anywhere in the world, Anne can customize a message of hope, inspiration, and transformation through real life stories of those who have overcome sexual traumas that will transform your audience and leave them wanting more.

Anne's speaking philosophy is to appreciate, motivate, and inspire an audience while coming from a state of hope and peace. Although sexual abuse is often a taboo subject, it is very important to empower those who have survived to move forward and share what they have done.

Anne Peters is a keynote speaker and a healing coach. To discuss how she can assist you or your organization, contact her at:

FindingYourHope.com
Anne@findingyourhope.com
(253) 225-3380